Light, Love, and Peace

Visits From Heaven

KATHY GRAM LAMM, PA-C

WENDY GRAM BRICK, MD

SILVERSMITH
PRESS

Published by Silversmith Press–Houston, Texas
www.silversmithpress.com

ISBN 978-1-961093-71-3 (Softcover Book)
ISBN 978-1-961093-72-0 (eBook)

This book is dedicated to our parents,
Carol and Ted Gram, and to all the angels
who made this book possible.

Contents

Preface

This book is not about miraculous cures but rather the miracles of messages and visits and visions of angels and heaven. It is to let those who hear the messages know that the future is that of wonderment and beauty and is not to be feared. It is to let those who are left behind with broken hearts know that their loved ones are in an amazingly beautiful, perfect and loving place.

We have been blessed by those who have shared these messages, and they have strengthened our beliefs and comforted us during our struggles. Because they have helped us and those we have shared them with, we hope they will do the same for those who are reading them.

Kathy:

I still remember it all so vividly... driving to my parents' house for what I knew would be my last visit with my amazing mom. She had survived a breast cancer diagnosis several years earlier and had returned to her normal healthy self. Just two months earlier, she and Dad, my sister and our families had been hiking in the Appalachian Mountains, and she had no trouble keeping up with any of us. No signs, no symptoms, and all was well. And then in the blink of an eye, it wasn't. The pain started, and we soon learned that her cancer was back with a vengeance and had metastasized to her bones and brain. And just like that, life changed. The happiness and laughter were replaced with overwhelming sadness. It felt like a horse had kicked me in the chest. Every morning, I woke up and hoped it was all a bad dream. But it wasn't, and it was the beginning of the end of the family of four that had always been the most loving, warm, happy haven for me.

Within days of getting the news, I quit my job as an Urgent Care Physician Assistant and started the four-hour drive to my parent's house. I would be staying for whatever time Mom had left and would help my parents through the most difficult and heartbreaking experience our family had ever been dealt. As I neared the house, I felt overwhelmed to think that the woman who was always looking out the kitchen window and running out to greet me would soon be gone. The person who loved and cared and taught and laughed and seemed invincible to me. How was this possible?

We did our best to stay busy and act normal, but we were crumbling inside as we watched her slowly fade. What do you do when there's nothing left to do? And how do you even start to say thank you and goodbye to the person who taught you everything when there aren't words to adequately convey what your heart wants to say?

In one of our last conversations, I asked Mom what she would say to God if she had the chance. After a short pause, she said, "I would ask if I did a good job." With tears in my eyes and a quavering voice, I assured her that she had done the very best job.

When Mom took to her bed to stay, she slept more, and we talked less. On one of her final days, she was resting comfortably, and I was sitting at her bedside reading a book when she enthusiastically yelled "Mom!!" She sounded so incredibly joyful and excited! I hopped up to see what had happened. She focused on me for a few slow seconds and looked as if she was ready to explain, but then she said, "You wouldn't understand," and she closed her eyes. And that was it. After a few days in a coma, she passed away. I had prayed and prayed for a different outcome. I was devastated. I was angry. Why hadn't God listened? Why hadn't anybody heard my prayers?

A few weeks later I started my new job as a Physician Assistant in Pediatric Hematology and Oncology. I wasn't sure if I would be able to handle working, let alone working with sick children. My sister assured me that I could. The staff knew my story and greeted me with open arms and gentle words, and I appreciated their kindness and understanding. But I was distraught, and although I was raised in the church, I found myself questioning everything. How could God let this happen to my wonderful mom? And these precious children? If He was out there, why wasn't He doing anything? I felt guilty about it, but I found myself doubting God. Not just His power or His choices but doubting His very existence. And just when I felt completely lost and at my darkest point did my journey to enlightenment begin.

Wendy:

As a young child, my greatest fear was losing my parents. I adored them. To me, they were perfect. We loved them so much. And they loved us unconditionally. I couldn't wrap my head around ever having to live life without them. And then I had to, and it hurt so much that I thought it would kill me. I felt like I couldn't breathe.

Grief and anger were a heavy burden. Grief over loss. Anger over what I thought were unanswered prayers. The anger eased somewhat when I realized that God answers prayers in His own way and in His own time. But the grief... not so easy. I know it's cliché, but it's true, great grief is the price we pay for great love. It was staggering. I felt that I couldn't move on, but I had to. I had a family, a child, and a career. I had also promised my parents that I would. But I needed to believe that I would see them again. I knew my mom believed that. But I needed a sign.

I vividly remember my first sign. I was driving home from work one day, about 8 months after my mom died. One of her favorite songs came on the radio, "Joy to the World" by Three Dog Night. It made me smile, which was something I hadn't done much of since I'd lost her. I said, "Mom, they're playing your song. If the next song is "Old Time Rock and Roll," (another of her favorites that she loved to dance to), I'll know you're here with me." Believe it or not, that was the next song. I had chills. But I had to push it. I said, "Wow, Mom. That was amazing. If the next song is "Tonight's the Night" I will 100 percent know that you're here with me." You guessed it. Rod Stewart starting singing,

"Stay away from my window . . ." I was stunned, ecstatic, incredulous. She was there. Oh, how I needed to know that! It was a turning point for me.

I guess that I've always been sure that we continue to "be" long after our physical bodies are gone. I've never questioned that fact. My faith tells me that. Even if you look at it only from a scientific viewpoint-energy is neither created nor destroyed, so I knew we must continue. But what happens when we continue in that next realm? I truly believe we will be with those we love again.

These stories that have been shared with us have helped us see glimpses of what lies ahead. They are beautiful and they give us hope. We hope that they give you hope as well.

Marcus
Visits With Grandpa

Marcus's family jumped at the chance to spend the day at the local amusement park. The tickets were a gift donated to the families who frequented the pediatric cancer center. It was a much-needed distraction from Marcus's difficult battle with cancer and would likely be his final outing.

Marcus, a 9-year-old cheerful, bright-eyed boy, was one of the first patients I met when I started my new job as a pediatric oncology physician assistant. When I first saw him, I noticed his beautiful smile, his infectious laugh, and his puffy cheeks from taking steroids. Marcus was there because he had a mass on his brainstem, and his brain tumor had no cure. His treatment was aimed at prolonging his life and would later focus on keeping him comfortable.

Marcus and his family had been looking forward to their family outing for weeks. By the time the trip rolled around, Marcus's condition had worsened, and he was confined to a wheelchair and required oxygen to keep him comfortable. Since they had limited seating in their small family car, I offered to drive to their apartment to pick up several of the family members. His mother greeted me with open arms and invited me into their small, but comfortable living room. I took my place at the end of the couch as I waited for Marcus to come out of his room. There were family pictures scattered around on the coffee table and end tables. I picked up a photo of Marcus and his oldest sister playing basketball. I just assumed that he had always shaved his head and had been a bit chubby. In stark contrast, I saw a thin, athletic young boy dribbling a basketball, his brown skin glistening at the edges of his thick afro. I still remember being surprised at myself for not considering how much he had changed since his chemotherapy started.

Marcus's mother gathered his things while his two sisters finished getting themselves ready. I could hear Marcus's sweet voice carrying on a conversation in his bedroom, though I couldn't make out who he was talking to. I guessed it was his father as I hadn't seen him yet. When his father appeared at the front door, I didn't give it much thought until I heard Marcus chatting again. I knew I would meet the mystery person shortly. As we loaded the oxygen supplies, purses, wheelchair, and various bags into the vehicle, Marcus's father carried the frail boy out and buckled him into his seat. His sisters slipped in behind him. I stood for a minute waiting for his bedroom guest to join us. His mother noticed that I was looking at the front door and asked if I had left something behind. I told her that I hadn't, but that I wondered if whomever Marcus had been talking to would be joining us. She gave me a smile, put a hand on my arm and said, "Oh, Marcus was talking to his grandfather. But since he passed away several years ago, he won't be joining us." I didn't know what to say and she obviously noticed the confused look on my face. "Ever since Marcus got sick, he has been seeing his grandfather standing in the corner of his bedroom. His visits have been occurring more frequently over the past few weeks. At first, we were concerned hearing Marcus's seemingly one-sided conversations. He would talk and then pause, and then answer or respond with a giggle. Marcus seems to be overjoyed with each visit and that makes us happy." I took in her words with a slight smile and nodded as I got in the car. I had never heard of anything like this before.

Several weeks after that day at the park, sweet Marcus joined his grandfather in heaven. It was my first patient loss and it hit hard. I grieved and wondered, "Is this really the job for me?" I had only known this young boy and his family for a few months, but I was devastated at having to say goodbye.

For several days and weeks after his death, I thought back to my visit to Marcus's home and the unusual exchange I had overheard. I had so many questions and I wanted to understand. Conversations with his dead grandfather? Had his disease made him see and hear things? Had his medications made him hallucinate? Was he really seeing his grandfather? What was going on?"

I was still having questions about my faith at the time and was feeling let down that the prayers for my mom had gone unanswered. And then Marcus's conversations with his grandfather made me step back and take pause.

Over the course of my career, many more beautiful encounters similar to Marcus's have been shared with me. While I didn't know what to make of it at the time, today I have no doubt that Marcus was having conversations with his grandfather, his comforting angel and visitor from heaven.

I remain thankful to this day for that experience and how it became the pivotal moment that opened the door to my healing journey and renewed faith.

Ella
Ella's Mission

Had the angels come to visit? That was a question I often asked patients who I thought were near the end of their lives. I was always fascinated when I asked and a patient would smile and reply, "How did you know?" I got this reply relatively frequently. The angel visits always comforted the patients, and it certainly comforted me to know the angels were around.

It was the end of a long day as I made my way to Ella's room, eager to ask her about the angels. I'd seen her that morning and knew her condition was declining but I'd been on my way to rounds and, sadly, didn't have time to chat.

I hurried down the hall, thankful that I now had some time to sit and talk with Ella. I stepped into her room, not knowing what to expect but hoping to hear that she'd seen the angels. I stopped in my tracks. The room was sweltering. My attention was quickly pulled to Ella. The elderly woman, lying in the hospital bed, appeared lifeless. "Is she still breathing?" I heard her take a raspy breath, almost in answer to my thought. She was frail and weathered. Her wrinkles were the sign of a full life, lived with laughter and passion for over 95 years. On admission, she had been about as spunky as a person with pneumonia could be, but earlier in the day that spunk had been replaced by fatigue and sleepiness. I had promised her I would return before I left for the night. Although I tried not to pick favorites, she was one of mine.

Ella and her family agreed that we would keep her comfortable, but we wouldn't use heroic methods to keep her alive. The pulse oximeter was beeping as it signaled that she was not oxygenating well. "Why in the world do we have this pulse ox on her when we're just trying to keep her comfortable?" I turned off the offending monitor and gently removed the sensor from her finger. She didn't move or give any hint that she knew I was there. I pulled a chair over to the bed to sit down and took her hand in mine. Again, she didn't respond, and I looked at her closely. The room was dimly lit by the evening sun and, until that minute, I wasn't aware that her skin had turned a dusky blue. I touched her shoulder to see if I could arouse her and noted that her skin was cool to the touch, even through her hospital gown. "No wonder they have the heat so high, she's freezing," I thought. Her breathing was slow and shallow, and I was so sad that I hadn't made it back to her room in time. She was such a beautiful soul, and saying goodbye would be difficult.

As I held Ella's hand, I looked around the room. Ella's daughter-in-law, Carol, who often spent most of her day visiting, was sitting quietly in the chair in the corner. She hadn't said a word since I'd entered the room and I'd been too focused on Ella to notice that we weren't alone. Carol had removed her cardigan and pulled up her hair. She looked at me with gratitude, that I'd cared enough to come sit with Ella. "She's not been awake since I've been here," Carol whispered. I nodded, knowingly. "I really don't think she's going to wake up," I replied. "I'm sorry to say this, but I doubt she'll make it through the night." Carol had tears in her eyes as she said, "She's lived a long, happy life. We're all thankful that she's comfortable and resting peacefully. What more can we ask?"

I was disappointed as I left the room and headed home for the night. "Why hadn't I asked her about the angels before?" I was sad that I'd missed my chance. Knowing her, she would have been excited to talk about them if they had visited.

Heading to rounds the next morning, I stopped at Ella's room to ensure that she was no longer there. I was right, the bed was empty. Out of the corner of my eye, I noted a movement on the other side of the room. Carol was still in her chair, and she smiled at me; she knew what I was expecting to see. I was confused by her smile and even by the fact that she was still at the bedside. And then I saw Ella sitting in a chair! Her hair was neatly combed, her eyes were sparkling, and she was smiling. Her skin was no longer blue and mottled but was now a rosy pink, especially her cheeks. She laughed when she saw my expression, which I'm sure showed how shocked I was. She exclaimed, "You didn't think I'd be here, did you?" I stammered to respond. I was stunned that this sweet woman who had been so close to death yesterday was looking well and sitting up in a chair today. How could that be? "You thought I died!" she said almost teasingly.

Ella beamed. "Well, as a matter of fact, I did die! And I

went to heaven! I was greeted there by my husband, my father and Jesus. They were all there!" Ella looked into my eyes as she emphasized, "And heaven was so beautiful! The colors of the flowers were so brilliant and so different than any colors I've ever seen." She waved her hands around her chair as if the flowers were growing beside her. "We don't have those colors here. I have no words to explain how gorgeous it was!" She smiled, "I was at peace, and I was so happy to be in heaven with my dad and my husband."

The smile on Ella's face then dropped and I could feel her happiness turn to disappointment. "Then I was told that I couldn't stay in heaven. I had to come back." She hesitated for a few seconds, recalling what had happened. "I was so upset. I begged and begged to stay. It was so wonderful being there with my family. I felt such peace and joy." Growing more pensive, she continued, "They told me that I had to come back because my sister is an atheist. I had to come back and tell her that there is a God and there is a heaven, and it was my mission to make sure she knew."

Ella looked at me, clearly irritated, and raised her voice, "I am so mad at my sister!"

I looked over at Carol, who was now quietly laughing, "This has been the conversation all morning. Ella is so upset with her sister." "I sure am!" Ella responded. "She's the reason I couldn't stay in heaven! I wanted to stay! I begged!"

I smiled at Ella. She was so energetic and passionate. I still couldn't believe that she looked so good when she was cold and blue just hours before. At the time, I'd never heard of anyone being close to death and actually visiting heaven. This was even more amazing to me than the angel visits. This was a visit to heaven! And she was given specific instructions!

Ella continued her amazing recovery and went home a few days later. For the remainder of her hospital stay, whenever anyone entered her room, she relayed her story of visiting heaven and having to return because of her sister. No matter how many times she told the story, she was elated over her visit to heaven and always so disappointed in her sister.

It's been almost 30 years since I met Ella. I've always wondered how that conversation with her sister went. I was certain she would fulfill her mission to educate her sister. But how would her sister respond? Would she be amazed by the colors? Would she realize she was wrong about God? How did that play out? I never saw Ella again so I couldn't ask her, but I have wondered about it many times.

What happened with Ella changed me. Although I had never doubted that there is a heaven, I really hadn't stopped to think about what it would be like or even consider that we all have a purpose here on Earth. At the time, I didn't know how many times I would hear similar stories from patients, but each time it solidifies my belief that we are going to see a wonderful and beautiful place when we eventually die.

I also know that I can still feel the happiness in my heart and the amazement I felt when Ella was telling me about her visit to heaven. I'd lost my own precious mother just two years before and I was thrilled to think of my mom meeting her family as she crossed over to heaven.

I've often told patients and friends about Ella and her visit to heaven. It always seems to help when someone is sad or grieving or questioning. It's one of the reasons we are now sharing our stories with others.

Chuck
I'm Good to Go!

A true "salt of the earth" kind of guy, Randy has no airs of superiority or self-righteousness. He is a pastor, a farmer and a forgiving and understanding man. He prefers to help and guide, and he leaves the judging to a higher power. He enjoys visiting with friends and those who attend his church, especially when they need a shoulder to cry on or just an ear to listen. He enjoys preaching and teaching, but he also enjoys just being there so his friends know they matter and they're not alone. People feel that they can be open and honest in his presence, and they often pour their hearts out to him.

Randy had known Chuck for years. Chuck was a confident, outgoing, and rambunctious man. He enjoyed life. If something was fun to him, he did it more than once, regardless of the consequences. His escapades never involved breaking the law, but they also weren't things he was now proud of. He typically greeted Randy with "How the hell are you?" and could often be heard saying, "When I die, I'll split hell wide open!" He felt that totaling all the good and bad he had done in his life, he was more than likely in the negative.

Randy repeatedly assured him that it was a "faith process" rather than a "points process" to get to heaven, and that nobody was tallying the good versus the bad. Chuck didn't buy it. He believed in God and heaven, but he still thought he merited going the opposite direction. And he was quite terrified of dying for that very reason.

When Chuck was ailing, Randy went to the hospital every couple of days to visit with him. Chuck would prop himself up in bed and the two would chat about anything and everything. Personal issues or solving the world's problems, it didn't matter. The chats were uncensored and filled with amusing anecdotes from the past or thought-provoking questions about the future.

On one particular day that will forever be vividly emblazoned in Randy's mind, Chuck greeted him at his hospital room door. His face was red and flushed, and he looked like the sun had burned him. Chuck was beyond excited to see Randy, and he couldn't wait to start talking. He was shaking and stuttering, and he couldn't seem to contain himself. Randy wasn't sure what to make of what he was seeing as he had never seen Chuck so energized and seemingly unable to control his emotions. Chuck very excitedly told Randy, "I'm good to go!" Randy stared at him for a bit, not understanding what the electrified man was saying. Chuck shook his head up and down, eyes wide, and said, "I'm going to heaven! Randy, I'm going to heaven!!!" The two men continued to stare at each other, both with wide eyes and mouths agape. Chuck then eagerly went on to explain that just prior to Randy's arrival, a brilliant white being had appeared through the window. He pointed to the spot as Randy tried to wrap his mind around what he was being told. Chuck, still stuttering, said, "He told me I'm good to go! He said God had prepared a place for me! For ME!! And I'll be there soon!" Randy was stunned, having never heard words of quite this magnitude before. Chuck further detailed the experience, "He" was beautiful and brilliant and light. And "He" had spoken to him right in that very room. "He" had assured him of his place in heaven and had eliminated his greatest fear. Chuck was so confident and elated. He was giddy and thrilled beyond belief. Chuck told the story over and over, and Randy was more than happy to listen. This time Chuck was the teacher and Randy was the student. Chuck had sins, but he also had faith. The two men talked late into the night about the events of the day. They marveled at how God was aware of Chuck's need for assurance that he was going to heaven, and how "He" magnificently provided that assurance, and at the time when Chuck needed it most.

Chuck died three days later and Randy presided over the funeral. Randy relayed the amazing experience that Chuck had shared with him, and he reassured Chuck's family and loved ones that you don't have to pretend you're good enough to get to heaven. Sometimes you just have to show that you need a Savior, and your Savior will show you the way.

A tribute from Randy:

> "A Tribute for my friend, Chuck.
> I remain both grateful and amazed God sent a messenger to assure my friend that his sins were forgiven. That an eternal home was waiting for his arrival. That his sin debt was paid

in full. The angel said, "I was good to go!!" Chuck was going to heaven!!! Chuck desperately needed to hear that message and truth be told, I needed to be reminded, too. It is always "unmerited grace" that gets us to heaven. We could never buy enough Girl Scout Cookies to pay for our sins! It's just not happening. We need our name written in the Lamb's Book of Life."

Jillian and Jeremiah
A New Friend

Sweet little Jillian and her big brother, four-year-old Jeremiah, spent countless hours at the Children's Cancer Center. She was there to receive chemotherapy treatments and he would tag along because it was too difficult for their mother to find a sitter for the frequent clinic visits.

The specialists at the cancer center did their best to provide a happy and playful environment for the long days that many of the children had to spend there. There were a multitude of games and activities available for the patients and their siblings. Jillian and Jeremiah loved playing and spending time together. They were both meticulous in their neatness, Jeremiah especially so. When he painted, all the paints were lined up neatly, and he always used brushes because finger painting was too messy. When they ate snacks, their little tables were spotless. They did not like messy hands, messy tables, or messy work areas.

There was a little girl named Maria who was being treated at the same time as Jillian. The two frequently shared the same chemotherapy schedule, and therefore were often in the infusion area at the same time. As fastidious and compulsively neat as Jillian and Jeremiah were, Maria seemed to relish being carefree and messy. In fact, Jeremiah called Maria "the messy girl." And Maria's little brother was equally messy, if not more so. When Maria and her brother left an exam room, it was a disaster, with smashed crackers and cookie crumbs everywhere. And when they played and did arts and crafts in the infusion area, there was a trail of paint, markers, glue and glitter everywhere. Although they had a wonderful time with their works of art, the path of chaos was quite upsetting to Jeremiah, which is why the children never played together.

Jeremiah grew very attached to the Child Life Specialist, Sharon, who was a favorite of most of the children at the cancer center. She played games with the children, painted and colored with them, and was the one who explained scary procedures and other medical terms to them in a way that made them easy to understand and not so scary.

Jeremiah was such a happy little boy that there was some concern that perhaps he didn't understand that his sister's prognosis was very grim. He soon proved everyone wrong when one day he drew a picture of the 3 of them— Jillian, Jeremiah and Sharon. In the picture, Sharon is crying, and Jillian is drawn above the other two. When she asked him why she looked so sad in the picture, he said it was because his sister was going to die, and Sharon would be sad when Jeremiah and his sister wouldn't be visiting with her anymore. Although saddened to hear his words, she was relieved that he seemed to understand the gravity of the situation.

Over the next few weeks, despite all efforts to cure the little girl, Jillian's cancer progressed. Over time, efforts went from trying to cure the cancer to trying to make her as comfortable as possible for as long as possible. During that time, the clinic visits became more frequent, and Sharon saw Jillian and Jeremiah at least weekly. On Jillian's last visit to the clinic, the difficult decision was made to stop all interventions because they weren't helping to improve her quality of life.

Amy, another child life specialist, was in the clinic that day and helped Jillian put her little handprints on paper so that her parents could always have them as a physical remembrance.

So weak that she couldn't sit comfortably in her car seat, the little girl was placed in her mother's arms in the back seat. Almost as soon as they arrived at their home, sweet Jillian passed away.

Although Jillian was gone, Jeremiah continued to "see" her. He told his parents about his frequent "conversations" with his little sister. He let them know that Jillian was very happy in heaven. One day, his mother overheard him laughing and talking, in what seemed another language, so she knocked on his bedroom door and said, "Hey buddy, who are you talking to?" He responded with, "Jilly said hi." He continued laughing and when his mother asked if Jilly had said something funny, Jeremiah very casually replied, "You don't need to know." He never considered that seeing and talking with somebody who had died was unusual. On occasion, Jillian's little musical potty chair would start playing. Jeremiah would hear it and say that it was his sister and that she still liked the musical chair. He loved when she visited.

About eight months after Jillian's passing, there was a

gala held to benefit the Children's Cancer Center. Everyone was there, including Jeremiah. His mother was a very active supporter of the cancer center. She loved and missed her precious Jillian so much and wanted to honor her memory by giving back. Jeremiah was very excited to see his old friend, Sharon, and to tell her what had been happening in his life. He told her, "I see Jilly all the time. She has friends, lots of friends! Just today she got a new friend that I would never have as a friend...the messy girl!"

Sharon was startled by what Jeremiah had just said because Maria, the messy girl, was in remission and was doing well. She was still receiving treatment, but her prognosis was good, so she couldn't possibly be the new friend that Jeremiah was talking about.

Later that evening, while still at the gala, Maria's oncologist pulled Sharon aside. He braced her as he told her the bad news. Maria had suddenly and unexpectedly died that day. Sharon was stunned! She stood shocked and stared across the room at the little boy. He knew. How had he known?! But he did. He knew that his little sister had a new friend in heaven, and Jilly was now friends with the messy girl. This revelation left little doubt that the conversations shared between the big brother and his little sister were, in fact, very real.

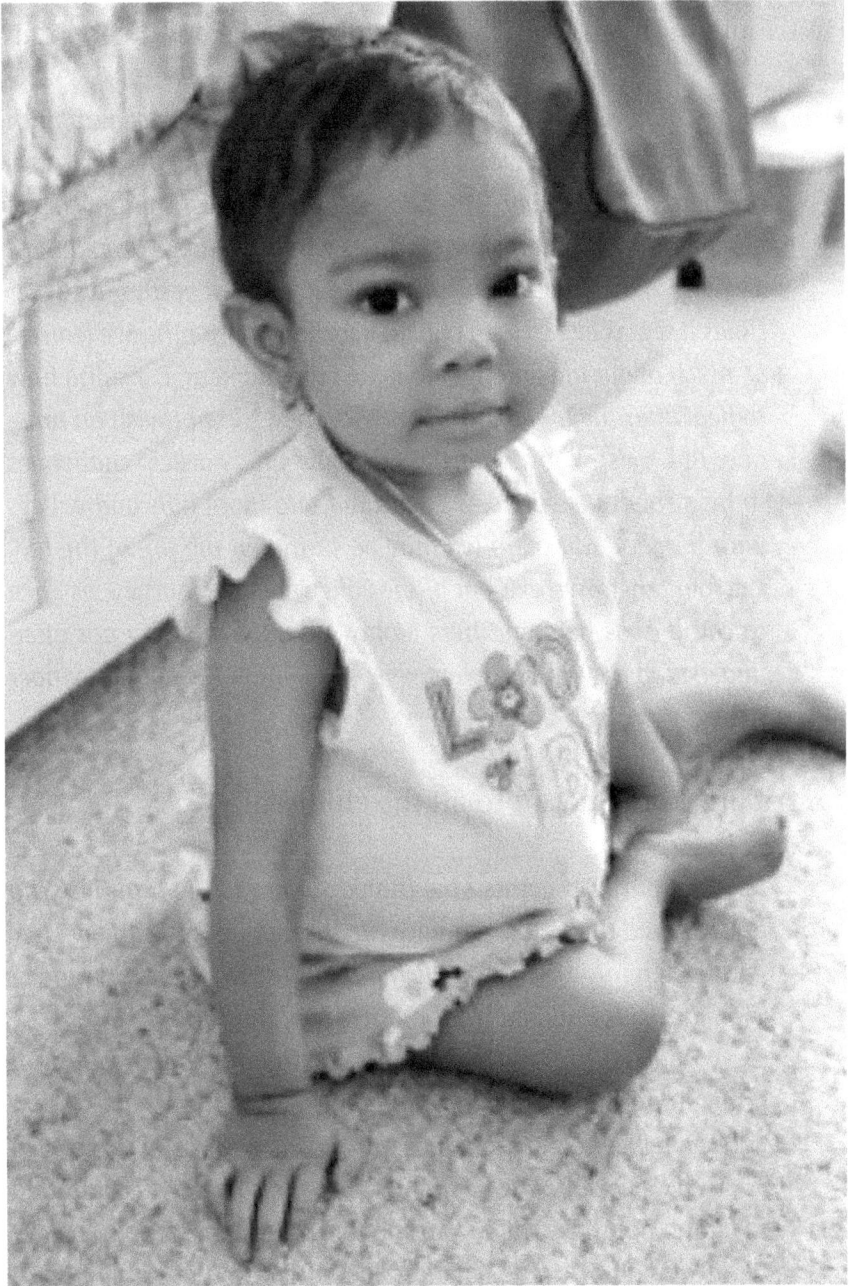

Jillian

A tribute to Jillian from her parents, Antoine and Keehanna:

The 13 months between diagnosis and transition seemed so much longer than it really was. I can remember it all vividly. The good, the bad, and the ugly. The relapses, the victories, and even the acceptance that Jillian's time with us was limited. It's been almost 15 years, and sometimes it seems like it was just yesterday. Other times it seems like so long ago. In her short 22 months, we learned so much about life and how to live in the moment. Learning how to heal after the loss of a child is a journey I do not wish on anyone. But I also know that the Lord gives his hardest challenges to his strongest soldiers. We ventured into those hills and valleys with her, and although we may be sitting on the top of the hill, she found her own exit out of the valley. Jillian's journey, as I like to call it, was hers and hers alone. Although we may not often understand it, we have accepted it. —Antoine & Keehanna Avinger

A tribute from Sharon to all the children:

I cannot put into words how thankful I am to the families who have shared their children with me throughout my career. They let me step into their lives during the most raw, heart wrenchingly difficult and beautiful moments of their lives.
They allowed me to bear witness to strength that I could not understand the depths of as an adult.
They helped me to see the beauty in this world and some even allowed a peek into the beauty of what's to come. I am comforted to know that they will be waiting for me, for all of us, in a place with colors that cannot be described because they simply don't exist here. And to Jeremiah, you were right, I missed you too!

Whitten
The Whisper

Whitten's leukemia had relapsed. After a 4½ year remission and reprieve from the constant battle with leukemia, it was back. The recent high school graduate was an old soul—genuine, unique and brilliant. He had been accepted to a number of esteemed colleges across the country and should have been heading off to start his freshman year at Rice University. Instead, he would require a bone marrow transplant to have any hope for a cure. A search ensued for a marrow donor, and friends and family were typed to see if they were a match. His sister, Lynn, who was just a year younger and who had a very close relationship with her brother, was found to be a perfect match. Whitten did his research on bone marrow transplant programs and their success rates, and he decided where he would have his transplant. The family traveled across the country and settled in for the long battle ahead. Lynn's marrow harvesting and Whitten's bone marrow transplant went without a glitch. And, although his leukemia responded favorably to the transplant, a fungal infection attacked his weakened immune system. Potent anti-fungal medications were added to his long list of medicines, and every attempt was made to rid his body of the infection. Inevitably, he was too weak to fight off the infection, and his condition continued to deteriorate. Early in the morning of November 6th, the family and loved ones were gathered at Whitten's bed and were told that he had little time remaining. He was receiving morphine to keep him comfortable, and his breathing was labored. The family was told that he "could go" at any time. His mother, Betty Lynn, and his father, Walter, were at his bedside, and Lynn was at the head of his bed. Hours passed without a change in his condition. The room remained quiet and free of distractions. Then, suddenly, Lynn felt a light above her and heard a kind, older woman's voice very distinctly calling from "high above" as if to call him upward. The voice was a loud whisper that sounded distant but was somehow very clear, and it repeated the call, "Whitten... Whitten... Whitten" three times. Lynn was looking down at her brother when she heard the voice, and she quickly glanced around the room to see who was speaking, but nobody seemed to be talking. Within the minute Whitten took his last breath.

Later that night the family returned to the house where they had been staying. Lynn and her father went outside and sat on a bench and stared out into the beautiful starry night. She had eagerly been waiting for the chance to talk about the voice she had heard in the hospital room. She asked her father, "Whose voice was calling out to Whitten?" He looked at her curiously. He had not heard a voice. He had no idea what she was talking about. She was stunned. She quickly went inside to ask her mother if she had heard the voice calling out to Whitten. She hadn't heard it either.

Lynn stood in disbelief, trying to process how she could have been the only one to have heard it. She had thought that everybody in the room had heard the voice calling out to Whitten.

Shortly after Whitten passed away, the family returned to their home in North Carolina. When they arrived at the house, many friends and family were there to embrace them. Lynn's Godmother had been part of a prayer circle for Whitten, and the group read daily from the Catholic "Mary Day by Day" prayer book. The woman told Lynn to read the November 6th message from the day Whitten had died. Lynn read the words, "You will be greeted at the gates of heaven by Mary." What comforting words they were to Lynn as she recalled hearing the woman's whispered voice beckoning to her brother.

For years Lynn wondered why her prayers for Whitten hadn't been answered. She had desperately wanted him to be cured. It didn't seem fair.

Then one day, her mother, Betty Lynn, told her about a dream she'd had, a dream she had desperately been praying for. In the dream, Betty Lynn, Lynn, and Whitten's girlfriend, were all standing on a boardwalk looking down at the beautiful, clear, Caribbean blue sea. The most incredible tropical fish were swimming all around the coral and urchins. And there was Whitten, swimming among them, underwater and never needing to come up for breaths. His eyes were open, and he was exploring everything there was to see, gliding through the water and physically well. This was especially poignant as he had always loved swimming and being in the water. And he was wearing his favorite light blue jeans, white t shirt and white socks. The three stood there just watching him, and Betty Lynn felt the peaceful-ness she had long been praying for.

Lynn heard her mother say, "God is good. God is Good!" And it suddenly struck her that she hadn't seen the whole picture. God HAD healed Whitten. He had just done it in His time and in His place. Her precious brother was healed and whole again in heaven!

Lynn is very confident of the voice she heard all those years ago. She feels that it was truly an incredible gift that she got to hear her brother being called to heaven. She and her mother are both so grateful for the dream that they both wholeheartedly believe was sent from Whitten to comfort them and give them peace.

Whitten with his family—Lynn, Betty Lynn and Walter

A tribute from Whitten's mother, Betty Lynn:

We had hoped and prayed so hard for a miracle to occur and for our precious, beautiful, brilliant boy to be healed. But our prayers weren't answered. Maybe God didn't hear them? Every night as I said my prayers I begged God to let me dream about Whitten; to give me a sign that he was ok and that he lives on. Many months later I received the most special gift and the answer to my prayers. A dream I will always treasure and never forget. It happened! The dream I had prayed for! I realized during those moments that God did answer our prayers. Not the way we had hoped, but he gave Whitten the best gift of all. The gift of eternal life. No longer did he have his battered body, but his spiritual life had begun. He could explore the world in a way that is completely beyond our understanding. Thank you, dear God, for making Whitten well so he could show your Son Great glory. There is not a single day that we don't think of and miss Whitten. In his 19 short years on this earth he accomplished an amazing lifetime. Until we meet again, my dear son, you will live in my heart always.

  I love you, Mom

  As written on Whitten's grave marker, "The quality of life cannot be measured by its length but by its depth."

Victoria
You Just Feel Him

Victoria was an adorable 4-year-old girl who loved wearing a crown and playing princess, even when she was in the hospital receiving chemotherapy. Despite her germ cell tumor initially responding to her rigorous treatment regimen, her cancer kept returning.

Her adoring parents tried to keep life as normal as possible for Victoria and her two brothers. The three siblings were all enrolled in a private school which provided the benefit of smaller, more individualized classrooms as they eased Victoria back into the school setting. Her cancer had caused several neurologic changes, including a facial palsy which affected her speech, and leg weakness which confined her to a wheelchair. The private school environment made it easier for the school re-entry child life specialist to educate Victoria's classmates on her condition and to help prepare them for her return to school. Victoria would attend classes in between her frequent clinic visits and hospital stays.

When Victoria and her parents would visit the clinic to discuss scan results or new treatment options, the clinic child life specialist, Sharon, would take Victoria to a different area to play games, make crafts or to talk.

During one memorable clinic visit, while they were playing a game, Victoria mentioned that she had seen Jesus in her classroom. She had never spoken to Sharon of anything like this before, so Sharon was surprised and curious, and she began asking questions. She asked Victoria whether there were certain times when Jesus was at the school, to which Victoria responded, "He's there all the time." She then questioned what He looked like, and Victoria informed her that, "Sometimes he looks like an old man, and sometimes he looks like a boy. He always looks different." Sharon asked Victoria how she recognized Jesus if He always looked different. The little girl replied, "I just feel Him. He feels like every color of the rainbow all at once, and then some colors that you've never even seen before. You feel Him." Victoria then asked Sharon to please return to playing the game.

Sharon eagerly looked forward to Victoria's follow up visit so they could continue their conversation. When they reunited, she asked Victoria if she knew why Jesus was in her classroom, and the little girl responded, "Because He's happy that I'm back at school." She said that He recently visited her when she was in the hospital and at her brother's soccer matches. Sharon asked what he looked like at all of those different places. Slightly exasperated, Victoria reminded Sharon that "It's what he FEELS like, not what he LOOKS like!" The beautiful colors that she felt when Jesus was near gave her a warm and happy feeling in her heart. Sharon asked Victoria if she knew why she could see Jesus when other people couldn't. She simply said, "Everybody CAN see Jesus, but I don't know why everybody doesn't. I'm just really happy that I can!"

Victoria with her mother, Elizabeth

Tribute from Victoria's mother, Elizabeth:
"Our Little Sunshine"

My firstborn was the cutest baby boy, and he was such a joy. When I was pregnant the second time and the ultrasound revealed it was a girl, I was so excited. She was the daughter I named and prayed for even before there was a double line on the pregnancy test. This was the child I had asked God for. She was a peaceful baby that grew into a spunky, sassy (in a good way) little girl. She had soft curly hair that I loved to put cute bows in, like my own little doll.

A little boy and a little girl. It was perfect. Until it wasn't. She was diagnosed shortly after her 4th birthday and our lives were forever changed. She was resilient, creative, and feisty. She fought cancer until it took her voice away in the end. There came a point when she felt that she wouldn't get better right before she died. I took comfort knowing she was never afraid because she had The Lord, she saw angels and would point to them as if we could see them, too.

We knew when she took her last breath that she was in the arms of her Creator. Though our hearts were broken, hers was whole again. She was our little sunshine.

Today, we miss the milestones that she would be experiencing had she lived, but for now we are left with imagining what it must be like for her now. We are thankful to have had the honor of being her parents.

Katie
Angels Among Us

Not long after Katie was diagnosed with cancer and started her chemotherapy treatments, she started noticing the most magnificent "colors" around her. They were amazing, but the five-year-old struggled to describe the brilliant oranges, reds, and yellows that she was seeing. She didn't understand why they were there or what they meant, but they made her heart feel happy. They were peaceful, warm and comforting, and they made her feel protected.

Along with the many unpleasant aspects of having a cancer diagnosis, one of the bright spots for many of the patients is the incredibly strong friendships that are formed along the journey. Any differences the patients might have are irrelevant when they are all united in their goals, and they are all extremely supportive of each other. Little Katie was no exception. She made many sweet friends at the hospital, but her very favorite was a teenager named Brandon. He was always so kind and patient with her, and the two spent countless hours together playing Candyland, Life, or just hanging out together while their mothers talked. Brandon was a huge Carolina Panthers football fan, and his favorite color was Panther blue to match his beloved team. Unfortunately, his brain tumor was very unpredictable, responding to treatment and then relapsing. After years of intermittent chemotherapy, his long battle ended. After he passed away, the families and staff were left devastated over the loss of the boy they had all grown to love. Katie, too, was shattered. Shortly after her dear friend passed away, Katie noticed a large blue aura around her. It didn't have a face, but Katie knew immediately that it was Brandon and that he was now her angel. She couldn't explain it, but she remembers with certainty that she knew right away that it was him. The colors finally made sense!! Once she made the connection, she realized what all of the beautiful, comforting colors were. They were her angels! In time, she understood that one of the colors was her grandmother and one was her great grandmother, and they had been with her throughout her entire cancer journey. "Like I said, I don't know how, it wasn't like their faces were visible, I could just feel it." Although Katie never lacked for visitors during her illness, the presence of her colorful angels kept her company and made her feel safe. Even after she finished her treatments and no longer required hospital stays, she could see and feel her angels nearby. "Even when I was cleared from the hospital and started living a normal life back at home, I saw them. Late at night when I closed my eyes and couldn't sleep, they were there."

In a discussion with Katie during her teenage years, she said, "Although I don't see my angels nearly as frequently as I did before, I still feel their presence and know they are watching over me. The colorful images are less of a vision and are more of a feeling of energy. I've never been a "super religious person," but I'm confident that we're being watched over, that God is real, and that there are angels among us."

She continued, "When I was little, I used to pat the side of my bed twice to call on my guardian angel. I don't remember who it was, since I couldn't see a face. I don't think it's anyone that I know or remember. But I can feel it. Feel him, I guess I should say. I would call on him so I wouldn't get a bad dream. Sometimes I still find myself doing it out of habit. Sometimes I do it just to feel safe. When I was little, it used to be colors, but now I can just feel it, like an energy."

Now in her mid-twenties, Katie doesn't feel the colors or angels like she used to. They have faded with the passing years. But she does remember the beautiful, vibrant colors and the peaceful comfort her angels brought to her when she needed them the most.

Katie

KATIE

Tribute from Katie's mother, Brigette:

After Katie started treatment and progressively grew weaker, she started to see angels. She would ask me "Mommy, do you see them? They're so pretty. So many colors." I have to tell you that it creeped me out a bit at first. She saw them most when she was sickest and most afraid. They brought her a lot of comfort. She would notice them, and you could watch her relax. It was as though someone had wrapped her up in a cocoon of love and happiness. I worried that they were there to guide her to heaven away from me, but over time, I realized they were simply there for her no matter what happened to her little body. And so, they brought me comfort as well. I tried my best to see them when she would point, but to no avail. When our sweet friend Brandon passed, she came to me the next morning and said he was with "her angels, Carolina Panther blue." I hadn't told her that he was gone, yet, but she knew. I don't think she sees them anymore, but she remembers them, and I know they are still with her. I have to believe that all the children fighting cancer have their guardian angels with them as well. I am so thankful the angels brought comfort to Katie. Katie's joy when the angels were with her brought immense solace to me.

Jacob
Best Buddies

So many feelings and emotions to deal with. Devastation. Disbelief. Anger. Numbness. Three months of what his parents thought were night terrors. Then worsening back pain and loss of appetite. Then a CT scan and a referral. Then the diagnosis. And then the devastation. Unimaginable devastation.

But little Jacob took it all in stride. The adorable 22-month-old loved nothing more than spending time at home with his mom and dad, but he made the most of the dreaded hospital stays and quickly wrapped the entire medical staff around his little finger. The funny little charmer learned how to wink when he was just three years old. He and his favorite stuffed animal, Nanook, would make their rounds, visiting with the nursing staff and winking at them because he knew it made them smile. He loved hanging out in the child life office and was known to occasionally check out 17 movies, even though the daily limit was two. He could be mischievous at times, and his mother remembers the morning he popped his oncologist in the jaw because he had awakened him from a cozy slumber. Although it didn't hurt, the physician, a father of five himself, had a heart-to-heart discussion with Jacob to let him know he couldn't just punch people in the face.

Jacob's mother, Chanda, had a co-worker, Jonathan, who was diagnosed with bone cancer within months of Jacob's neuroblastoma diagnosis. Although there was a twenty-year age difference between them, the two enjoyed hanging out together discussing Star Wars, Transformers and other fun topics. Chanda loved that Jonathan was a big kid at heart and that both families were able to share their journeys together to make the load a little lighter for everyone. It was such a sweet friendship and Chanda loved watching the two friends laugh and play together. Jonathan was always so patient and gentle with Jacob, and Chanda and Jacob both sensed his deep faith in God. Jonathan bravely faced several surgeries, including an amputation of his leg, but his attitude remained positive, and he continued to inspire those around him. Despite the surgical and chemotherapeutic attempts to cure him, Jonathan eventually succumbed to his cancer. One of the last things Jonathan said to Chanda before he died was "Get to know God, Chanda." What a truly inspiring young man. Chanda worried what the news of Jonathan's passing would do to Jacob. She knew he would be devastated. When she found the courage to tell him, she braced for his reaction. She then smiled as the little boy enthusiastically and confidently told her that Jonathan was now in heaven with Jesus.

Over the next several months Jacob intermittently asked his mother questions about Jonathan. "Does Jonathan have to have chemo in heaven?" "Does Jonathan need his wheelchair in heaven?" "Can Jonathan fly in heaven?" Chanda doesn't know what answers she gave, but she does remember the afternoon that Jacob saw Jonathan again.

It was about a year after Jonathan had passed, and Chanda and Jacob were at home in their kitchen making cookies. Jacob stepped away from the counter and started walking down the hallway toward his bedroom but stopped mid stride. Chanda watched as Jacob stood motionless in the middle of the hallway. The afternoon sun was setting through the living room window, and it appeared that Jacob was staring outside. She asked him if everything was okay, but still, he didn't move. Anxious by that time, she began walking toward him, again asking if he was ok. He turned toward her, smiling excitedly and said, "Mommy! I see Jonathan!!" Chanda's first reaction was that Jacob was seeing a shadow from the sun or some sort of glare on the window, but she recalls suddenly feeling chills and a calm settle over her. She replied, "Wow! Jonathan is here? Where is he?" Jacob pointed to the oversized chair that was near the window and matter-of-factly said, "He's right there, Mom!" Chanda looked at the chair and although she saw nothing, she said, "Hi Jonathan! Thank you for coming to visit us!" Jacob, still staring at the chair shouted, "Mommy! He's standing up! And he has both legs!!!" Chanda remembers an eerie feeling, like a presence in the room with them, but she didn't feel at all afraid. She recalls acting like what Jacob was seeing was nothing out of the ordinary—like it was no big deal that he was seeing somebody who had gone to heaven. And then just as quickly as it happened, Jacob was on his way back down the hall and Chanda was left standing in awe.

After another year of chemotherapy treatments, radiation, multiple extensive surgeries, a stem cell transplant and a monoclonal antibody clinical trial, with completely broken hearts, Jacob's parents said goodbye to their sweet boy. They had tried every possible treatment that gave any hope for a cure, but the cancer was relentless.

Jacob made a tremendous impact on every person who knew him. And although his parents love him beyond measure, and miss him every single day of their lives, they remain amazed by their little boy's unquestioning and absolute faith, and his mother is so grateful that she was able to experience his excitement over his angel visit with his buddy Jonathan.

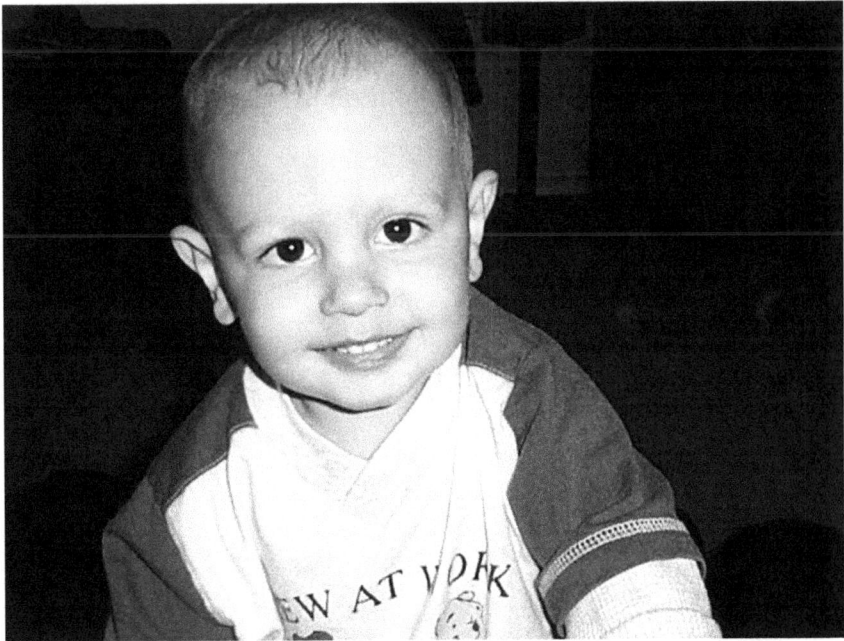

Jacob

A tribute to Jacob from his mother, Chanda:

As I reflect on this memory, I am reminded of God's grace. I am so thankful I was able to share that amazing experience with Jacob, and that he was able to see Jonathan happy, healthy and whole again. I believe that children are able to see things that adults can't, and I truly believe they can connect with angels or spirits or souls. I believe children are closest to angels, they are pure in form just as they are. And I also know in my heart, that is exactly what God intended.

There is never a day that passes without a reminder of Jacob in some shape or form. Remembering the steps leading up to the diagnosis, and the entire cancer journey are not easy on our broken hearts.

Jacob succumbed to neuroblastoma December 18, 2003. Even though it has been over two decades since his passing, I hope that by reading this story of a little warrior with a pure heart and soul, it brings you peace.

Warren
Across The Meadow

It was breakfast time and Warren was seated at his usual spot at the dining room table. Each morning, he enjoyed his breakfast there in front of the large picture window, gazing over a beautiful, rolling meadow with lush woods on either side. Although an elderly man, Warren was in good health other than the slow, but expected, decline for a man of his age. He and Annie had been married for decades. Their life had its fair share of trials and tribulations, but they had weathered them together as a team. They relied on each other for everything, and every bump in the road just seemed to make them stronger. They knew how blessed they were to have each other. They looked forward to starting their mornings together, relaxing, and enjoying each other's company.

Annie was in the kitchen one morning making their breakfast when she heard her husband shout, "Annie, come here quick!" The urgency in his voice compelled Annie to drop everything and run to his side. When she reached him, she found Warren sitting completely still, eyes wide, and mouth open in astonishment as he stared in awe out the window.

He was mesmerized. She quickly followed his gaze to see what was causing his excitement, but she saw absolutely nothing out of the ordinary. He remained transfixed as he gazed out the window. He was overjoyed as he pointed. His eyes grew wider and without moving them from the scene, he excitedly whispered, "Look! Coming across the meadow!!", as if to be sharing a special secret with her. He then paused and in a slowed and hushed voice that sounded somewhere between disbelief and pure wonderment, choked out the words, "Is that not the most beautiful thing you have ever seen in your life?!" His voice caught with emotion and tears welled in his eyes. He continued to stare, awestruck.

Annie moved around the table, trying to find a better view of what Warren was seeing. She looked back and forth between her husband and the meadow, trying to figure out what she was missing. Still, she saw nothing other than the lovely field, and she remained puzzled by what had him so captivated.

She then remembered that their breakfast was still cooking on the stovetop, and she rushed back to the kitchen, hoping the oatmeal hadn't burned. She prepared their bowls and drinks on the tray and headed back to join Warren. She entered the room hoping she would finally be able to see what had made him so joyful. She stared out at the field as she walked toward the table. Clearly something spectacular was out there and she was determined to find it. As she approached his chair, Annie asked, "Is it still out there?" She was greeted with silence. "Do you still see it?" Again, silence. She put down the tray and hurried to her husband's side. She was shocked to find that in the short time she had been gone, her beloved husband had passed away. Suddenly and without warning. He was gone. Annie was heartbroken. He had been her world. Her everything.

In the weeks and months following her husband's death, Annie frequently revisited that morning. Warren's excitement and awe at the spectacular sight, that only he had been able to see, brought her immense comfort. She had never seen such delight and pure joy as she had seen on his face just before he died. Could it have been angels coming for him? She felt sure of it. Warren had lived with a strong Christian faith and his life had been well lived and fulfilling. Annie found great solace in knowing how completely joyful he was in the final moments of his life. What a magnificent gift it had been for both Warren and Annie.

Kim
The Visits

Kim tried to ignore the pain in her jaw and neck. She was singing in the church choir and wasn't about to call attention to herself. The pain began radiating down her left arm and she grew more concerned. "I'm only in my fifties, I can't be having a heart attack!" Unfortunately, the pain worsened, and she began to feel heavy pressure in her chest. By that time, she knew that no matter how much she tried to deny it, she was having a heart attack. For whatever reason, she didn't tell anyone at church about her symptoms, nor did she ask for an ambulance. She just got up and left. "I remember the sensation of leaving my body and watching myself from far overhead, as I drove from the church to my home and then on to the hospital. I even watched myself navigate through my house in search of an aspirin." She paused as she looked at me, seeing my amazement. "It didn't even seem unusual. I could see the car moving down the street and I could see myself in it." She did find it odd that, even though she lived in a large city, there were almost no cars on the road and every stoplight on the route to the hospital was green. It was as if a path had been cleared for her.

In the Emergency Department, she was immediately taken to a room and evaluated. A heart monitor was attached, and EKGs and labs were performed which showed that Kim was having an acute myocardial infarction. As she continued to float over her body, watching calmly as the events unfolded, she was rushed to the cardiac cath lab for emergent heart catheterization. She recalled the entire procedure clearly. She felt immense comfort and was grateful that she had made it to the hospital in time and vividly remembered the comfort she felt as she received treatment. "The peace I felt was like a blanket, wrapping my entire body." Through it all, Kim watched from above. After the procedure was complete and she was stabilized, she was moved to a room in the ICU. It was only then, when she was resting and her condition was stable, that she felt herself being pulled back into her body, where she remained for the rest of her hospital stay.

Kim came to see me a few months after her heart attack. As she relayed her story, she was calm and matter of fact. It didn't seem to concern her at all that she'd had a major medical problem or that she'd been hovering above her body as she watched the action below.

I, however, was fascinated. I had heard of people floating above their bodies, and I had even had another patient tell me that she had left her body and watched herself being resuscitated, but that patient was "coding" at the time and had no heart rhythm. Kim was actually watching herself as she was driving her car, walking through her house, and undergoing a procedure. When I asked her about this "out of body" experience, and why it didn't seem amazing to her, she told me that, while she did think it was amazing, she was no longer surprised when it happened. "Since the death of my husband, I've had similar experiences, and they always bring me great peace and tranquility."

She went on to explain that her husband had died suddenly when he was a young man, leaving Kim behind with 3 young daughters to care for. "I was distraught when he died. I was so scared and overwhelmed. What was I going to do without my husband?"

She was afraid to be in her house at night and felt that she couldn't adequately protect her girls. She remembers wanting a security system but being unable to afford one, so she prayed for protection for her daughters and herself.

One night, in the depths of despair, she went upstairs to her bedroom and began fervently praying. She prayed for help with her daughters and for protection for her grieving family. As she sat on her bed, her attention was drawn to the stairway in the hall. She was transfixed as she saw a "band of light" rolling up the steps. Although it was difficult for her to describe, she said it was "rolling like fire" and its appearance was magnificent. The band was about 12 inches wide, and its colors were indescribable because "we have no colors like that in this world." The band of color rolled up the steps and down the hall and into each of her daughter's rooms and then whirled into her room and began swirling around her, wrapping her bed in a colorful, safe cocoon.

As she sat there, astonished at what was taking place, three "angels" suddenly appeared at the foot of her bed. "They came out of nowhere and had almost human forms, but I couldn't make out actual faces. There was a translucent quality about them, but they were solid forms. They were like nothing I've ever seen before." Kim was mesmerized as she watched the angels gently sit beside her on the bed. They were silent and didn't say a word, but she knew in her heart that they were angels. "There was no fear at all. Suddenly and almost magically, I was at peace. The fear of life without my husband was gone. The sorrow was gone. All anxiety, distress, and doubt were gone when the angels were present." She was at total peace, and it was at that point that she knew everything was going to be okay.

Comforted, and knowing that her house and her little family were protected by the angels, Kim fell asleep and slept like she hadn't slept since her husband died. When she awoke, the angels and the band of light were gone, but the peace she felt was still there. She knew the angels had been sent to be with her and help her and that they'd been sent in answer to her prayers.

Although she never saw the angels again, she did have the feeling of sudden and complete peace in subsequent times of great anxiety or stress. "So, when I was having my heart attack, and was watching myself from above, I just thought it was my angels helping me navigate to the hospital. I was thankful and not questioning."

A few months later, Kim returned for follow up. She was eager to share her most recent experience with me and this time she was thrilled at what had happened. "It starts out sad, but trust me, it gets amazing. My mother died recently. While we are heartbroken, we've been expecting it for a while. She was quite elderly, and she had been disabled mentally by a severe stroke that she suffered a few years ago. We hadn't really been able to talk to her since the stroke. Her physical condition had recently been in rapid decline and her doctor had prepared us that she was not expected to live much longer. Imagine our surprise when she suddenly became lucid and had the mental ability of a 40-year-old! For the week prior to her death, we had our mother back. It was an unexpected gift, and we were so happy to be able to share stories with her and tell her how much we loved her."

Although she had recovered mentally, her mother's over-all medical condition continued to worsen. Kim recalls the day her mother died. "I was lying in bed with my mother, and I was holding her in my arms when she passed over. As she passed, I was suddenly "with her" as she transitioned to heaven. It was as if she pulled me with her. I was seeing what she saw as she arrived in heaven. It was incredible! I watched as those who had gone before her lined up on two sides of the "pathway" as they prepared to greet my mother. She then started moving along the pathway, escorted by her Master, Jesus. Although there were many waiting to welcome Mother to heaven, they waited patiently and "held back" as there was one that was going to be the first to welcome her. I could sense the excitement from all the loved ones that were lined up. From the end of one of the lines came my brother, Phillip. We hadn't seen him since he was a teenager. He had passed over when he was only a teen, after being brutally injured in a farm machine accident. I watched as Phillip was running as fast as he could to reach our mother. He was joyous and so eager to welcome her. I heard him exclaim to her, "You're not going to believe the things you're going to see!" I felt my mother's joy!

That was the last I saw or felt as I was quickly pulled back to my mother's bed. I had seen all I was allowed to see, apparently. It was a thrill I'll never forget. To know that is what awaits me when I eventually cross over to heaven is a gift I will carry with me forever. It is all love and joy and peace. What a wonderful thing to look forward to!

Nora
So, How Was It?

It was a long flight from London to Australia and David knew they might not have the luxury of time; his mother, Nora, lay dying in an Australian hospital. His daughter Emily was en route from London, hoping to arrive in time to say goodbye to her beloved grandmother. David, a physician, had agreed with his mother's wish not to perform resuscitation should she die, allowing her to pass away peacefully. She had no fear of dying; she had lived a great life, had a loving family and friends and had traveled the world. She was very close to Emily and was looking forward to seeing her granddaughter one last time.

The morning that Emily was to arrive in Australia, David entered the hospital room to find his mother cool and blue and obviously close to death. He quickly realized that her oxygen tubing had been clamped by the wheel of the bed during the night, and she wasn't receiving oxygen. He now had a dilemma: let his mother pass away peacefully, as he had agreed, or restart the oxygen flow in the hopes that she would awaken and be able to see her granddaughter one last time. Because he knew that they wanted to say their goodbyes, if possible, David rolled the bed off the oxygen tubing. As he waited to see if his mother would respond, he noted the pink color return to her face, and she slowly became responsive.

David, who freely admits that he isn't sure what happens after death, curiously asked, "So, how was it?" His mother smiled and replied, "It was so peaceful. I was met by a bright light. A bright light and a welcoming warmth. There was absolutely no fear and I only felt peace." She knew that David had made the decision to revive her. She let him know that she was pleased he had given her the chance to say goodbye to her precious granddaughter.

Emily arrived in Australia later that day and made her way to the hospital. She and her grandmother were both very grateful that they were able to say their goodbyes.

A few days later, David was at his hotel when the hospital called. His mother was near the end. He rushed to her bedside to be with her. As he held her hand, he whispered, "It's ok to let go....we will be alright." After Nora passed away, her family recalled the experience she had and felt comforted knowing that she had passed over to the peaceful, warm, welcoming light. What an incredible gift they'd been given as they said their final farewell to the woman they loved so much.

Punky doodle
The Noble Dog

Punky Doodle was an enormous dog with a personality that equaled his size. His human was Ann, and she knew from the start that the 240-pound English Mastiff would be the perfect pet therapy dog. He was known throughout the children's hospital for calming, loving, and bonding with the sick children, especially those with chronic illnesses who were frequently hospitalized.

One day, while Ann and Punky were in the pediatric intensive care unit, a physician asked for their help. There was an eight-year- old girl named Courtney who had recently been diagnosed with an illness that would require frequent hospital stays. The doctor believed that if Courtney befriended Punky, the hospital stays would be a little less scary and a lot more fun.

When Courtney first saw the gigantic dog, her eyes were huge and she was obviously terrified. She hid under her covers and peaked out only to make sure the dog wasn't getting any closer. She wanted her grandmother to make him go away. But the elderly woman, who was raising Courtney, talked with Ann and insisted that she and Punky continue visiting until Courtney was comfortable with them. She believed it would be beneficial for her granddaughter. Ann was hesitant, but she persisted with the visits as grand-mother had requested. Slowly but surely the child's fears dissipated and she began to trust the lovable dog, and with each visit Ann watched as the bond grew between the two. In a very short time, the giant dog and the tiny girl had grown to love each other. Every time Ann was preparing to visit the hospital she would ask, "Do you want to visit Courtney?" and the lovable dog would immediately stand up and head to the door.

Following one of Courtney's surgeries, the doctors requested that she get out of bed and start moving around. She stubbornly refused to walk if her canine friend wasn't at her side, so Ann and Punky visited frequently to encourage her to ambulate. Ann recalls seeing the little girl walking down the hospital hallway, gown open in the back, arm outstretched above her head as she held tightly to Punky's collar. The gentle giant walked slowly and deliberately, sup-porting Courtney as the two made their way down the long corridor.

In addition to being recognized as Punky's favorite friend, Courtney was also well known for greeting every visitor to her room with a little southern drawl and the same ques-tion, "Will you dye my hair?" She would describe the bright white/blonde hair that she longed for to anybody who would listen, and then she would repeat the question, "Will you dye my hair?" The dirty blonde/brown color of her hair was clearly not what she desired. The hospital staff joked about it and found it entertaining that she asked everybody the same question, no matter who they were.

Despite the frequent surgeries to patch the issues with her intestines, the recurrent obstructions and many setbacks took too big a toll on her worn body, and the precious little girl passed away the day before Thanksgiving.

Shortly before she died, Courtney confided in Ann that her Uncle Bob had come to visit her and had described the beautiful room she would have when she went to heaven. She noted that his first visit was to her hospital room several months earlier, and that he had visited more frequently in recent weeks. Not knowing who Uncle Bob was, or whether other family members were present when he visited, Ann mentioned his comforting visits to Courtney's grandmother at the little girl's funeral. The woman was stunned and noticeably shaken at hearing Bob's name and that he had visited Courtney. After taking a few minutes to compose herself, she shared that Bob was her first-born child and that he had died before Courtney's mother was even born. The pain of the loss had been so great that she had never spoken of him to Courtney's mother or to Courtney. The fact that Bob had come to visit Courtney had come as a tremendous surprise but was very comforting to her grandmother.

Punky continued visiting with the children at the hospital through the end of the year. In early January, his health rapidly declined. After several veterinary visits and with no hope for improvement, Ann made the extraordinarily difficult decision to have her beloved companion put to rest. When they arrived at the animal hospital, the veterinary staff filed out of the building and lined the walkway to honor the noble dog. He carried his green frog in his mouth and shook hands with each of them, as he did with all of his human friends. He was so loved that the veterinarian laid behind him and hugged him as he passed. Ann was completely devastated and couldn't bear to share the news with anyone, so she drove home and sat alone in a quiet, dark house.

The next day the phone rang, and when Ann answered, a woman screamed, "WHEN DID HE DIE?!" Ann was startled and confused and asked who was calling. The flustered woman said, "I'm sorry, Ann. This is Courtney's grandma. Punky's gone, isn't he?! I'm so sorry! I didn't even know he was sick!" Ann was surprised to hear the woman's voice as they hadn't spoken since the funeral. And what in the world was she saying?! Grandma told Ann to sit down, and she went on to explain.

"Courtney and Punky came to visit me last night! It wasn't a dream, it was real!! I recognized Punky even before I knew my girl. She has her platinum blonde hair now!!" She went on to share that Courtney had said, "Tell Ann that I love her, and I miss her. I have Punky and I'll take good care of him. Thanks for sending him!"

Courtney then went on to explain to her grandmother, "You need to live your life! There's so much to do here. Stop worrying about me! When you worry, it ties me down." Grandma described hearing children's laughter in the background. She went on to say, "Courtney and Punky started to run off but then they both turned around at the same time, and Ann, I swear that dog smiled at me!!" Then having completed their mission, the two sweet friends turned and ran to join the other children.

As the news of Punky's passing spread, an incredible arrangement of flowers lined the front porch and steps of Ann's home, showing just how loved and respected the amazing dog was. Ann still misses and often thinks of her sweet canine companion, but she knows he is continuing his job as the most amazing therapy dog and best friend in heaven.

Punky Doodle

A tribute to Punky from his person, Ann:

Punky Doodle was an English Mastiff. We trained for and participated in the Pet Therapy programs at different hospitals, rehabs and group homes. He was a 238 pound love bug. Because of him, I was blessed with the opportunity to meet so many lovely souls that I would've never had the opportunity to meet otherwise. He truly was a once in a lifetime, and I look forward to seeing him again. Thank you for all of the precious memories, Punky, I love you.

"You think that dogs will not be in heaven? I tell you that they will be there long before any of us!" Robert Lewis Stevenson

Gene
The Presence

A massive stroke at the age of 38. Not unheard of, but certainly very bad. Gene was unconscious as he was rushed to the nearest hospital. In the Emergency Department, his family was given the grim news that he would probably not make it through the night. Despite the poor prognosis, they wanted to give him the best chance to survive, so he was transferred to the ICU in a larger hospital in a nearby city.

Although the family tried to remain hopeful, the doctors told his wife that if Gene lived, his life would never be the same. He would probably be paralyzed and would likely never leave his bed. The situation was heartbreaking for his family. He was so young and so were his children.

Gene recalled waking briefly after being transferred to the ICU. He prayed, "Dear God, please don't let me die! I have 3 kids that need their dad!" As he prayed, a white figure appeared in front of him, comforting him and promising, "Gene, you're going to be ok." He then lost all awareness.

Gene received excellent care in the ICU and, very

unexpectedly, his condition began improving. He was moved out of the ICU to continue his recovery. His wife and his family were overjoyed. He slowly regained movement in his arms and legs, and soon after that he began communicating. His recovery was nothing short of a miracle.

He told his wife about what he had witnessed in the ICU when he had asked God to let him live. He explained the glowing white "presence" and how it made him feel peaceful, warm and reassured. His wife was skeptical. She didn't understand how he could have seen the white presence. She told him that he had been unconscious for several days after his stroke and had not been awake at all during that time. He could not have seen anything in that room, let alone a white presence. Gene was undeterred. He knew what he had seen and what he had felt.

Gene then shared his account of the white presence with his physicians. They agreed with Gene's wife. It was impossible that he had regained consciousness during the time in question. Gene was adamant about what he'd observed. He then relayed an account of the day in question. He gave specific details of the events that had taken place in the room when the white presence visited him. He described doctors and what they were doing. He described the nurses. And he described the family members who were present in the room and what they were saying. He knew where they had been standing, and even what they were wearing, down to the tiniest of details. How could it be?

His wife and the doctors were stunned. However, they all confirmed that his details were quite accurate. They had not seen the bright white presence that had visited Gene, but they were now convinced that it had been there. Gene had been able to see everything that was going on in the room, even though he was unconscious, and his eyes were closed.

Gene recovered fully and lived to the age of 78. He loved to tell his story to others and share with them his strong faith in God. He hoped that others would come to know the love that is shared with each of us. Gene was confident that it was God who had healed him. Remembering that bright white presence was a great comfort to him throughout his life.

Bob's tribute to his father:

In memory of Dad.

I watched a man who, in September of 1971, had a massive stroke and was not supposed to live through the night, and he lived. Then, when he was never going to be able to get out of bed, he did. Then he was never supposed to get out of his wheelchair, but he did. Then after 6 months and 3 weeks, he walked into the factory where he worked and returned to his full-time job where he worked another 18 years. He died at age 78, having lived another 40 years after the stroke that almost took his life. His faith in God, his faith in Jesus, and his absolute determination to live made a lasting impression on his family and friends. I am forever thankful he was my dad.

After my dad died, I was walking through a parking lot at 6 o'clock in the morning. I was feeling low, and I was missing my dad. There was only one other person in the parking lot, and he was about 25 feet in front of me. Suddenly, there was a booming, massive voice that said, "He's ok. He's with me." I quickly looked at the guy in front of me, expecting him to have heard the voice and be looking at me, but it was clear that he hadn't heard what I had heard. That message was for me alone. My dad was ok. And he was with Him.

Brandon
Papa!

After a seemingly endless series of tests were performed to evaluate the new onset and rapid progression of his symptoms, one last study, a head CT, was performed. Brandon was just 13 years old when his brain tumor was discovered. He endured rigorous chemotherapy and radiation treatments, but the cancer was unrelenting. At the age of 16, his cancer had progressed and there were no remaining treatment options. His mother, Anita, remembers the pain of knowing that her sweet, wonderful child was not going to survive the horrible nightmare he was going through. She felt that, as his mother, she should have been able to protect and shelter him from his fears and help him be well again. She painfully recalls having to tell him that there was nothing else that could be done to cure his cancer. She comforted him as she gently told him that he would be going to heaven, and that it was an unbelievably beautiful place. Brandon was afraid of dying, so Anita reassured him that his Papa would meet him in heaven and the two would be together until she and his father could be with him again. She wasn't sure if he would really see Papa, but she hoped her comforting words were true.

Brandon's condition worsened and when he was too weak to climb the stairs to his own room, he took over his parent's bedroom on the first floor of their home. He woke up early one morning and told his parents to get showered and ready because he felt that it was the day that he would go to heaven. They were overwhelmed with emotion, but they began preparing themselves as he had asked them to do. While they were moving about, Brandon asked them if they could hear the music. They stopped and listened carefully but heard nothing. In fact, it was completely quiet. Their inability to hear the beautiful music frustrated Brandon, and he continued questioning them about it for over an hour. As quickly as they started, the questions stopped.

He then asked his parents to stop what they were doing and to sit with him on his bed. Something was happening! Brandon was lying in bed and although his eyes were closed, he told them he was seeing a light. Selflessly they told him, "It's okay. Go to the light." Brandon suddenly raised his hands toward the ceiling, lifting theirs with his. They looked at each other without saying a word, both feeling that a heavenly presence was in their midst. Suddenly they heard the most beautiful sound of birds singing. It sounded like thousands of birds! With his eyes still closed, Brandon asked if they could hear the birds singing. They assured him that this time they could hear the beautiful melodies that he was hearing. As difficult as it was for his parents to say the words, they gave him permission to "let go" and begin his journey to heaven. With a big smile on his face, Brandon said, "I see Papa!" They were overcome with emotion and gratefulness hearing Brandon say those words. Knowing that Papa was the one who would escort their precious son to heaven brought immense peace to his parents. Then, abruptly, all of their hands dropped, the birds stopped singing, and Brandon's eyes opened. Brandon looked up at the ceiling and started asking, "Why am I still here, God? I want to go to heaven. I want to go!" He was frustrated and impatient to continue his journey. After a short time, he was able to relax and enjoy visiting with his loved ones for another day. His parents found great comfort in knowing that Brandon was no longer afraid of dying and that Papa was close by and waiting to lead their son to heaven.

After his death, his parents looked forward to the time when they would all be together again. Since that time, Brandon's father has joined his beloved son in heaven. Brandon's mother and sister know that one day they will all have a beautiful reunion in heaven, but until that day they find comfort in knowing that Brandon is with his father and his Papa in heaven.

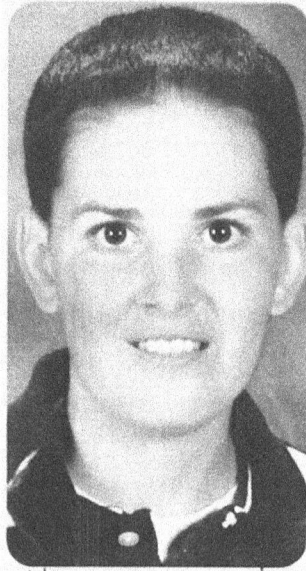

Brandon

BRANDON

A tribute from Brandon's mother, Anita:

Brandon was the one who made me a mom, something I had dreamed about forever. He was his dad's and my pride and joy, and he was the best big brother to his sister, Brooke. He was diagnosed with medulloblastoma (brain tumor) at the age of 13 and after battling for three years, he passed away at the age of 16. During those three years he became a hero and an inspiration to so many people, and he touched so many lives with his will to fight and live. He was known for his smile that could light up a room. Brandon's last wish, and a promise that we made to him, was that he would never be forgotten. We let him know that the impact he made in his short life will never be forgotten. On his marker it reads—Always Remembered... Never Forgotten.

Brandon had a special angel, his Papa, already in heaven when he got there. And sadly for all of us who are left behind, Brandon also has his dad with him in heaven now. Brandon, my only son and the best son I could ever ask for, taught me to live life to the fullest and to be the best person I could be. He is my special angel.

Libby
Poppy and Coco

Life was going great for Josh and Barb in March 2013. At 35 and 32, they had more than they could dream of. They had a new home, successful careers, a beautiful baby boy, Will, who was 7 weeks old, and a beautiful, sweet, spicy, funny, 2½ year old daughter, Libby, who was flourishing and loved her new brother. They were surrounded by loving family and friends and were overjoyed in their marriage and young family. And then, what they initially thought was a simple fever quickly spiraled into the worst nightmare imaginable.

Libby was immediately rushed from the doctor's office to the hospital and admitted to initiate chemotherapy for her newly diagnosed leukemia. The first round of treatment didn't work. Another, more potent, regimen was given. And still no response. Her rare form of leukemia was aggressive and relentless. The next step, a bone marrow transplant, initially seemed to be a success, but on day 98 the horrific nightmare resumed. Her leukemia was back. A new experimental therapy at the NIH, but again, to no avail. On May 8th, 2014, they said their final goodbyes to their precious Libby.

The following story about Poppy and Coco is written by Libby's mother, Barbara:

When Libby was about 2, Poppy and Coco entered our lives. In our eyes, they were Libby's imaginary friends. To Libby, they were her sisters, they were the babies in mommy's tummy, they were her friends. She went to their weddings, she talked to them on the phone, she played with them, she showed us pictures of them on her phone, she talked about them all the time—in extreme detail. "Who did you play with today?" "Poppy and Coco." "Who are you talking to?" "Poppy and Coco." "Are you going to have a sister or a brother? "Two sisters—Poppy and Coco."

This was purity of heart—a child's imagination. This was the highest level of playing pretend, or so we thought. I never had an imaginary friend, so I wasn't really sure how it worked. But I did know our Libby was beyond brilliant and could dream up anything. But one question always struck me about Poppy and Coco—where on Earth did Libby dream up their names? They weren't in books we read, cartoons we watched or stories we told. We didn't have friends or family with those names. They weren't baby talk names that one would concoct. I asked her teachers at school, and they, too, were perplexed. We didn't have an answer. We attributed the names to Libby's imagination. What other answer is there? But can a 2-year-old really dream up names she has never heard? I don't believe so.

We didn't give Poppy and Coco much thought again until much later, at least a year after we'd lost Libby. Then, Poppy unexpectedly re-entered our world. Sitting around our dinner table one Wednesday night, 20-month-old Will blurted out "Poppy, Poppy, Poppy" seven or eight times.

Josh and I just looked at each other, and back to Will—stunned. Had Poppy come back to us—unannounced, out of the blue, without warning? As always, more than ever, she was welcome in our home. We wanted to ask Will questions but didn't want to fuel whatever was happening in that moment. We didn't want to put ideas in his head, or feed whatever was happening—we wanted it to be as real as it could be, so that our experience could be as rich as his—if that was possible. We had never mentioned Poppy to Will, we hadn't talked about her in at least a year. Tears sprung to my eyes—I began weeping actually, almost short of breath. Chill bumps popped up on my arms, as the ideas ran wildly through my mind – what could this mean?

Will didn't mention Poppy again that night, or for several more months, and neither did we, but we certainly thought about her. I asked Josh's parents if they had mentioned her to him when he was living there—no. I asked Kathleen, our nanny—no. I even asked his teachers if they had been talking about puppies at school—no. Again, just like when Libby first spoke of Poppy, there was no answer.

I recalled a conversation I had earlier that summer with my friend, Amy. She had had a childhood imaginary friend, whom she recalls as very real. Her mother's stories of Amy's imaginary friend sounded very similar to what we experienced with Coco and Poppy. And Amy's mother's theory? Not imaginary friends at all, but angels. Guardian angels in the midst of our children. Beautiful. Perfect. Poetic. And as I have come to say about many things of this sort—WHY NOT? What is the harm in believing that Poppy is an angel? No harm, not if it helps me believe, helps me know I will see my Libby again, helps me dream of better days to come. WHY NOT?

This set my mind spinning. Coco and Poppy entered Libby's life when she was about 2; 8 months before she was diagnosed. So, I choose to believe that they were Libby's angels in our midst, surrounding her as she prepared to fight. WHY NOT?

Weeks after Will mentioned Poppy, it happened again. Will and I were playing in the playroom, and he was talking on his toy phone. I asked, like I always do, "Who are you talking to?" His first answer was "Chiefy," his second "Poppy." I stilled my reaction so that I was careful not to power his imagination (although I wanted to jump up and down with excitement), and I asked, "Where is she?" His answer, "Heaven." Really—could this be happening again? WHY NOT?

Again, we said nothing after that to Will about Poppy – we wanted so badly for this to be real, and for us to know that it was, we couldn't feed him anything. Two-year-olds repeat everything, and we needed, no, were desperate for and hungered for, this to be real.

And then a third time—the most amazing—again at the dinner table. Will was chattering away and pointed to the picture of Libby, Josh and me that was taken before he was born. "Momma, Libby," he said. "That's right," Josh said, "And where is Libby?" We have told Will from the beginning that Libby is in Heaven. Typically, when we ask him where she is, that is his trigger response. Libby equals Heaven, so if that had been his response, we would not have been shocked, but that is not what came out of his mouth. He very matter-of-factly, while stuffing his face with mini meatballs said "Home." I froze in my seat and observed as Josh carefully asked the same question again, with the same response, and then a follow up question—"Home with who?" "Home with Poppy." Holy moly! Josh and I stared at Will, then at each other. I could tell that Josh was more moved this time—more than the other times, and I felt it too. I, again, started bawling. I even had to leave the table, and squat down on the floor to catch my balance.

And then, of course I started analyzing—was Libby with Poppy in our home? Was Libby telling Will that she was home in Heaven with Poppy? Was she telling him not to worry about her because she was home—meaning Heaven? Did Poppy tell Will that she was with Libby and they were home? Was Poppy now Will's guardian angel, as she had been Libby's? WHY NOT? WHY NOT? WHY NOT?

And so again, I choose to believe. I have to. I have no choice. These extraordinary moments were a miraculous gift. A tidbit of our Libby. A piece to tuck away and pull out on our lowest of days. Why Not??

To me, there is no way to explain the moments, but as a piece of the supernatural. A glimpse into where she is, a peek into a world unknown to anyone on Earth, a prayer request granted, a wish come true. I wish I could describe these better, as my words are paler than pale in comparison to what we have experienced, but I have tried.

This story was difficult to tell, as words don't do it justice. A poem would do it no justice, nor would a song or a painting. As creative as artistic geniuses are, there is simply no technique available to capture this type of experience. These are the experiences you long for after losing someone you love, these are tidbits that help you believe, that strengthen your faith, that help you sleep, that help you hope. They may be tiny, they may be out there, but to a Momma and

Daddy who long for any glimpse of their baby girl, they could not be bigger.

Libby with her parents, Barbara and Josh.

A tribute from Libby's mother, Barbara:

> *You will never be forgotten sweet girl. You were beautiful, funny, smart, strong, spicy, witty, and lovable.*
>
> *You didn't just make us parents, you made us better parents. You taught us how fiercely we should love, how passionately*

we should live our lives, how we should advocate and fight for our children.

Through your journey we learned what devotion looks like, what love really is, how important it is to show up, how people all around us are struggling, and perspective in so many ways. Let us never forget how life can change so quickly. You were a happy, healthy little girl until one day you weren't. We were a joyous, growing, thriving family until we weren't.

How can it have been 10 years? Love you baby.

Cheri
The Light

Libby's grandmother, Cheri, vividly remembers the last few days of her darling granddaughter's life. They were in the ICU and little Libby was in a coma. She hadn't opened her eyes in days when her parents asked if Cheri would read, "If you Give a Mouse a Cookie." It was Libby's favorite book. When Cheri began reading, Libby opened her eyes, turned to them, and smiled. It would be the last time they saw that beautiful smile, as she lapsed back into a coma.

The following day the family gathered together, and the hospital room was filled with so much love for Libby. Cheri's husband, Scott, prayed for his granddaughter and the rest of the family. Libby was then taken off life support and placed in her parents' arms so they could hold their precious daughter one last time. At that very moment, Cheri saw an incredibly bright column of light shine down in the corner of the room. It was so intense it was as if a canned light had exploded. Cheri wondered why someone had turned on such a bright light in the otherwise somber, quiet and dimly lit room. The bright light went away as quickly as it had come. While being held in her parents' loving arms, sweet Libby passed away. As she passed, Cheri saw a second burst of intensely bright light shining down in the middle of the room.

After Libby was gone and many of the family members were out in the hallway, Cheri walked over to the corner of the room to see what had created the burst of light. Much to her surprise, there was no overhead light, no canned light and no other light source of any kind in the places where she had seen the columns of light shining. She stood and questioned what she had just witnessed. "Was it an Angel? Was it Jesus?" Astonished, she turned to look at her daughter, Callie, and exclaimed, "You won't believe this!" Before she could explain, Callie said, "What? The bright light in the corner?!" Wow! They had both seen it! It was as if an angel had come to carry Libby to heaven. It was such an incredible comfort to both of them.

As Cheri looks back on all that transpired, she knows that she was meant to be there to help support Josh, Barb, and Libby during those impossibly difficult days, to help with Libby's brother, Will, as well as to share her love and support with her other children, Callie and Clay, and their children.

Cheri recalled the bright light she had witnessed on the day Libby died and was reminded of an experience that occurred many years earlier when Libby's father, Josh, was born. Cheri presented to the emergency room in labor. The physician in the ER evaluated the mother-to-be and urgently informed the staff, "We need to move fast and get this baby out quickly!" Cheri then recalls leaving her body and "flying" above them, watching from overhead as her baby boy was delivered. It was as if she was watching a movie! It was her first baby, and she didn't realize at the time that not everyone experienced delivering a baby in that way. She would later come to understand that it had been a special gift for her to be able to experience her delivery in that extraordinary way.

Years later, Scott and Cheri moved to Charlotte, NC. She had three young children, a husband whose job required him to travel, and she hadn't made any friends in her new town. Her family, friends, and entire support system were all back in Texas, and she felt incredibly alone. She was struggling, and she spiraled into a depression. She wondered about her purpose and if she was even needed.

One Sunday, Cheri was in church and the choir was singing. She remembers hearing their words, "For everything there is a season, and a time for every purpose under the heaven." She was gazing at the choir, and although there were no stained-glass windows behind them, she saw beautiful colors appear. And then, in what seemed like viewing a beautifully colored "movie," she saw Jesus approach a little girl and gently "pull her up." As they began walking hand-in-hand, Cheri realized that the little girl was her. As she watched from behind, the two walked together toward something brighter. Jesus then sat down, and she felt Him wrapping His arms around her. She had the immediate and intense feeling that everything was going to be okay. Prior to seeing the "movie," she had felt like she had been looking into a dark abyss. And then she suddenly felt a total lightness, as if the darkness was immediately lifted and she was pulled back. Her depression was instantaneously gone, and she began weeping. She would never feel that dark depression again. Her "very real encounter with Jesus" changed her life. It was the most powerful and indescribable feeling of love she had ever felt.

As she looks back over her life, she truly believes that it is by God's Grace that she was there for her family when they needed her the most. She is so thankful for her prayer warriors and the incredible love and support she has felt throughout her life. She remains beyond grateful for her wonderful husband, children and grandchildren, and she lovingly remembers her sweet Libby, the smart, thoughtful, athletic, adorable little girl that she misses so very much.

A message from Cheri:

> As I reflect on the times that I have struggled in life, I can see God's divine providence in my life story. Whether I realized it at the time or not, His hand has touched me in the worst and best of times. He works everything out, works in me and through me, and works for my good.
>
> These stories are my stories of the most intimate moments with HIM. I share them to give others hope when all hope seems lost.

Josh and Kelli
Swing sets

Two of the happiest, kindest, and most thoughtful children in the world. That's how anybody who knew them would describe Josh and Kelli. Both were also battling leukemia, although they had different types that required different therapies.

When Kelli was first diagnosed and admitted to the hospital, she noticed that many of the children were confined to their rooms because their blood counts were dangerously low, which greatly increased their risk of infection. She, too, was restricted to her room because the initial round of chemotherapy was aggressive in an attempt to wipe out her leukemia cells and get her cancer into remission. She decided to make cards for each of the children on her unit, to encourage them and to help brighten their day. All of the children enjoyed receiving their greetings, but sweet Josh, who had been hospitalized for weeks, was ecstatic to receive mail from a new friend. The appreciative boy returned the favor by making a cheery card for Kelli, to make her smile and to thank her for her kindness. She was excited to get his response and to know that she had made a difference in his day. And so it began.

A bond of thoughtfulness formed between the two children. They seemed to enjoy their differences as much as their alikeness, and they both appreciated the traits that made each of them unique. The fact that Josh was an outgoing, talkative 9-year-old boy and Kelli, a quiet and shy 6½ year old girl, made no difference to the two. He was determined in anything he put his mind to, focused, observant, and so loving and gentle to others. She was an old soul, wise beyond her years, logical, funny and prayerful.

They loved making each other happy with upbeat notes or sweet messages relayed by their nurses or their mothers. Occasionally, they would gather their money to buy small gifts for one another from the dollar store. Their mothers enjoyed talking to each other in the hallways and going on shopping expeditions with specific directions from their children for the purchases they were to make. Even though the two children never met in person, they shared so many messages, pictures, and stories with each other that they felt like true and dear friends.

In addition to their compassionate side, they both also shared a great sense of humor, and they loved to make people laugh.

Josh's mother, Yvonne, still laughs about the morning Josh was in his hospital bed and hatched a plan to scare me by faking that he was asleep. I crept into the room as quietly as I could and very gently laid my stethoscope on his chest. As I was listening to the slightly hurried beat of his heart, he loudly yelled "BOO!!" Wide eyed, I stumbled away from the bed as Josh and his mother erupted in laughter. Several nurses quickly poked their heads into the room to see if everything was okay, and Josh squealed with delight as he told them of his prank and of how he surprised me. The mother and son talked about it for days and rolled with laughter each time they retold the story.

Kelli's mother, Angel, remembers the first time her daughter was losing her long, beautiful locks of hair. During one of Kelli's initial hospitalizations Angel remembers being jolted awake from a nap after hearing a loud "Mom!" The concerned mother quickly jumped up and saw that Kelli had taped the long strands of fallen, brunette hair to her upper lip to form a fu Manchu mustache. Kelli broke into uncontrollable giggling at seeing the shocked look on her mother's face, which in turn made her mother burst into laughter.

Josh and Kelli loved hearing the sounds of laughter coming from each other's rooms. They wanted nothing but good things and happiness for each other.

Unfortunately, Josh's leukemia did not respond to the chemotherapy and his cancer progressively worsened. He often talked about heaven and wondered what it was like. What would it look like and who would be there? What would there be to do in heaven? Was there singing in heaven? So many questions. One of the things he enjoyed more than anything in the world was playing on swing sets, so one of his most frequently asked questions was, "Do you think there will be swing sets in heaven?" It was a very important question for him, and he expected some thought behind the answer. Sweet Josh continued to bravely endure the long and difficult treatments in the hopes of a cure, but at just nine years of age the sweet little boy passed away.

Kelli's leukemia went into remission, and she remained cancer free for over a year. Sadly, her cancer returned, and she was sent for a bone marrow transplant. She received the recommended treatment and remained hospitalized to see how she would respond to the transplant. One morning, she woke her mother and was excited to share that Josh had visited with her during the night, and he had given her a message to share with his mom. She ecstatically relayed to her mother, "Josh is very happy! He wants us to know there really are swing sets in heaven!! I got to see him swinging and he was so happy!!" She was thrilled to have received this beautiful message.

Kelli's leukemia didn't respond as hoped to the transplant. She continued to fight, but when her fragile, exhausted body could no longer continue the battle, the sweet little girl passed away.

What wonderful little lights the two incredible children had been. Perfect examples of how to live life. Share as much joy as you can, be considerate of the struggles that others are dealing with and laugh every chance you get.

Our hope and belief are that Josh and Kelli are reunited in heaven and are happy and carefree, laughing and playing together on the swing sets in heaven.

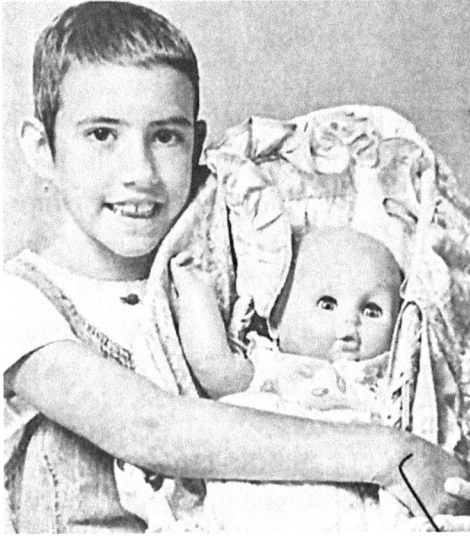

Kelli

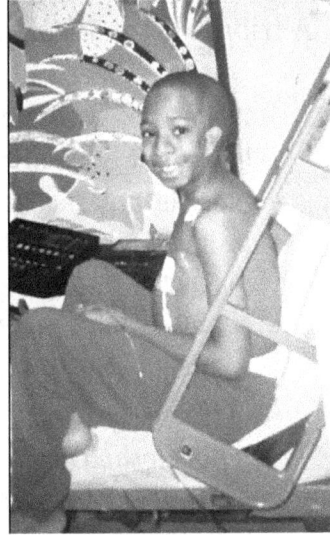

Josh

A tribute from Kelli's mother, Angel:

Although Kelli was only with us for 8 years, she impacted us all. Whether it was her friend from 2nd grade who messaged me almost 20 years later to let me know the ripple effect of Kelli's life, and how it led her to pursue a life as a chaplain on a hospital's cancer unit. ~To a father thanking me for my daughter's courage and sacrifice for what doctors have learned from our children's journeys, that are the reason his son is alive today. ~To her brothers who remind me every day of her through their love, compassion, and life choices in helping others. ~To me, Kelli's mother, who prays every day to be a better person today than I was yesterday. She showed us all how to step into and live our lives in God's light. ~Until we meet again, my beautiful miracle girl. Love, Mom

A tribute from Josh's mother, Yvonne:

When we heard the message from Josh about swing sets in heaven, it gave his father, Adlai, and I great peace to know that our precious little boy kept his mind on heavenly things. Josh wanted other children to know that everything was going to be okay. "Heaven ain't a bad deal!" Josh had great peace in knowing that, if God gave man the ability to make fun things here on Earth, just imagine how much He has in store for them in heaven!

How Joshua loved everyone. Just to see his doctors, PA, nursing staff and visitors come through the door, made his day. We believe Joshua made a great impact on everyone who came across his path. To all those special people, again we say, "Thank you, for great is your reward in heaven!"

Patsy
Standing In the Doorway

We got the call at 6 pm. "Critical patient on the way. Massive MI. Do NOT let the team leave the cardiac care unit (CCU)! "My heart raced. I was the intern on call in the CCU that night. Thankfully, the rest of the team hadn't yet left for the day. What did I have in store for me? I had no idea what to expect; this was my first night as an intern. I glanced at the clock on the wall, thinking about the patient on the way. I knew her name was Patsy because the outside hospital, where she had initially presented, had faxed her records ahead for our review. They'd tried to stabilize her but were losing ground fast. Her only hope was at our high-level cardiac unit.

Suddenly, the automatic doors to the CCU crashed open. The EMTs were doing chest compressions as they raced down the hall and into a room. I watched as the gurney sped by. The patient was mottled and gray. Was she even alive? Because the EMTs had been doing CPR the entire trip, she had her eyes taped shut to prevent them from drying out. At the time, I didn't understand why they were taped, and it made me uncomfortable as I wondered if the patient knew what was happening. Or was she so critically ill that she didn't even know what was going on?

The EMTs transferred Patsy to a bed and our team immediately took over the effort to save her.

Because I was a very new intern, I had no role in trying to resuscitate Patsy. I watched from the doorway of the room as my attending and fellow physicians worked diligently to get her heart into rhythm, only to have it stop again. "We have a rhythm! Rhythm gone!" This went on for what seemed hours and Patsy fluttered in the balance of life and death. Although everything during a code is fast paced, as I watched from the doorway, it was as if time was barely moving. I watched the faces, heard the words, saw the monitors but I wasn't really a part of the action. Almost like a movie.

I probably only remember that "code" so vividly because it was my first night as an intern, my first night in the CCU and my first code. Terrifying, but exhilarating. 30 years later, it's still etched into my memory. The thrill of getting her heart beating again and then the disappointment when the rhythm was lost, time and time again. All I could think was, "How am I going to keep her alive if they all leave for the night." Everything in my being wanted to run right out the door.

Eventually, Patsy's heart rhythm was stabilized and she made it through the night. After recovering for a week or so in the hospital, she went on to have successful coronary bypass surgery. I helped care for her during that week of recovery but Patsy and I never spoke of that night that she was so close to death.

A few years later, I was working in a different hospital in

the area and stepped onto the elevator. I held the doors as others followed, including a woman who continued to look at me as she moved to the back of the elevator. She was beautiful. Her eyes looked like Elizabeth Taylor's. I didn't know her, but she was obviously a visitor in the hospital. All of a sudden, she called out, "Dr. Brick!" I had no idea who she was until she exclaimed, "It's Miss Patsy!"

She was so excited as she recounted to all of us on the elevator how she had "died" the night of her heart attack. With great clarity she described how the doctors were working on her as she hovered over them. "I was floating above the room, watching them work on me. I wasn't seeing with my eyes though. It was warm and peaceful and calm to me, and I wasn't scared at all, even though I knew the people in the room were working to save my life. I remember sensing that most of them thought I was going to die. It felt like I was feeling all the emotions in the room, and I could feel that they all wanted to help me." She continued to recall, "As the doctors would get my heart restarted, I would be pulled back towards my body and then as they started to lose me again, I would float higher in the room. She then looked at me and said, "And I remember you standing by the door, watching as they fought to save my life. You never moved!"

And she was correct. I never moved. I was too afraid to move.

Everyone on the elevator was listening and they were all clearly emotionally moved as Patsy told her story. The doors opened. I stepped off, followed by a number of others. I turned around to continue my conversation, but the doors were closing, and Patsy remained on the elevator. I couldn't let her go without knowing more so I ran down the hall and up the steps, hoping she would exit on the next floor. I searched that floor and the next but didn't find Patsy. I wanted to continue trying to find her, but I had pages to answer and patients to see. I was so upset and wished I'd had more time to talk to her, to ask her how she felt and to see what else she remembered. Almost 30 years later, I still remember my heart jump as she described things that she couldn't possibly have seen with her eyes. They were, indeed, taped shut.

Todd
Messages From Heaven

Todd was a happy, strong and vibrant 17-year-old when he was diagnosed with stage 4 Ewing's sarcoma. The earth-shattering news of his disease did not stop him from living and enjoying his life to the fullest, even though he was dealing with chronic pain and enduring rigorous chemotherapy and radiation treatments. His determination, strength and remarkable sense of humor were inspiring to everyone who knew him. He could often be heard repeating his mottos, "I don't have time for cancer" and "I'll never give up."

Todd's contagious laughter and witty sense of humor brought lightness to the otherwise dark reality of his battle. His goal became not only to survive the ordeal, but to help find a cure. He noticed how little publicity and research went into Ewing's sarcoma and hoped to gain more attention for it and other lesser-known cancers.

Todd fought his battle with great dignity for 18 months.

While the family was establishing a memorial fund in Todd's name, they learned of the V foundation, which was founded by Coach Jimmy Valvano during his own battle with cancer. They were extremely impressed with the foundation and how it operated. But for them, it was personal. When they learned of Jimmy's motto, "Don't give up. Don't ever give up," they were moved to tears as they recalled Todd's pledge to "Never give up." They subsequently formed The Todd Bucher Foundation*.

When Todd's mother, Linda, heard about our project, she shared their story. The messages she received from Todd, through a neighbor of his grandmother, Dorcas, helped her survive her own grief and move forward with her life. She hopes this will help others as they navigate their own journey.

The Messages:

Elsie was a neighbor and acquaintance of Todd's grandmother. She believed in the power of daily meditation. On August 16, 2000, approximately 11 months after Todd passed away, she received an unexpected message during her meditation.

"Hello, I'm Todd."

Elsie knew she perceived things a bit differently than others but was still startled to hear this voice. She tried to remain calm as she responded, "I don't know anyone named Todd. Todd who?"

He responded, "Todd Bucher. I did visit her."

Although Elsie didn't quite understand what he meant, she responded, "I believe you."

Todd replied, "Thank you."

Three days later, Todd returned for a longer visit.

He said he needed to reach his mother and couldn't get through to her. He knew she was suffering, and he wanted her to know that he was fine, happy and rested. He could be at peace if his mother wasn't so sad.

Elsie said, "But I don't know your mother."

Todd replied, "No, but you know my grandmother. I've come back to ask you to get a message to my grandmother. I've tried to reach her, but I got a busy signal. I'm asking you because you can hear me."

Elsie told him that she needed to get the courage to do it.

Todd responded, "If you ask for the courage, you will get it. Thank you."

The following day Todd's message was,

"Hello, this is Todd. I'm counting on you to help me get a message to my mother. I'm fine, I'm happy, I'm rested. Please pass the message along through my grandmother, to my father. Thank you."

The very next day, Todd came in a more forceful way, with a bang.

"Don't give up. Don't ever give up."

Elsie said, "I am hesitant, Todd."

Todd said, "You can call my grandmother today. You have the courage now. Ask her to call my father and have him tell my mother that I am fine, I am happy, and I am rested. It will help both of us move on. Don't let me down."

Elsie called Dorcas that afternoon and relayed the message from Todd. Dorcas called Todd's father, Tommy, that night.

Tommy approached his wife, Linda, and gently relayed the message, "Your boy is trying to get in touch with you." She cried and shook all over and wanted him to stop speaking because she thought it was a cruel joke. Then she began to feel a strange calm, and as she calmed, she realized that no one who loved her would be so mean. She agreed to listen and remain open-minded, but she was still very skeptical.

Over the next few days, Todd's messages continued.

"I have a great family. When you see my mother, please give her this message. Tell her that her grief will be lifted. She will begin to feel joy again. Simple acts will let her know I am nearby. She will begin to see that all is not lost but she needs to work on her thoughts. She must release the negative and seek positive energy. It will take a while, but it is her job to get it. Life is too full for her to be down. Life is to be fully enjoyed. Please tell my mother this when you see her." He then told Elsie that she would be a positive energy for his mother. "Thank you, Elsie. Don't give up, don't ever give up."

When Dorcas called Elsie to tell her how grateful the family was for the messages, Elsie let her know that she had received another visit from Todd. Elsie was not surprised to hear that Todd's parents would be making a special trip to visit that weekend, and that she could share the message with them face to face.

That weekend, Todd said, "Yes, I'm back." He told Elsie that she would be fine visiting with his parents that day and that he would be there, too. He thanked her for being able to speak for him. He said it was a great day.

Elsie asked, "How do you think your mother will take this?"

Todd replied, "She will cry, but she will be fine. I think she can handle it."

Elsie asked him, "How about your dad?"

He said, "He will be grateful. He needed a hand with this. Thank you"

That day Todd's parents met with Elsie and talked for over three hours about Todd and his messages. Todd's father asked Elsie to say the words, "Thanks buddy, I love you!"

Todd came to Elsie that evening. "I cannot thank you enough for how much you have helped me. It was so good to see my family, to hear what you told them. The meeting went so well. It will make my mother be better and it makes me feel so much better. You told her everything I needed her to hear and she can now look up. And Dad... gosh, I love him. I heard what he said. I told you I would be there. As for my many friends, I am still with them, I cheer for them and I love them. He ended by saying, "I am quite peaceful now. I thank you with all that I have."

A few days later, Elsie was awakened in the middle of the night. Todd wanted to clarify that he is always with his sisters and they were included when he said that he loves them all. He said they needed to release any negative energy and they should not be upset that they had not heard from him and that he would find a way. He said their sibling bond was very special. Elsie told him that his mother would be having lunch with his best friend, James. He said he knew and looked forward to being there to listen to their conversation.

Elsie reached out to let Todd's mother know that he could tell that she and his friend, James, were doing better, and to tell James to be careful driving in the traffic. Todd's mother called James but got no answer. When he returned her call, he told her that he had been driving in heavy traffic and there had been several accidents along the route.

October 23, 2000

"Hello Elsie, it's me, Todd."

Elsie greeted him and asked how he was.

He replied, "I am great. My mother has improved, and I am proud of her. I am proud of all of my family. I send my love to my family, every single one of them." He continued, "I am able to visit my mother through dreams because she is free of negative thoughts and is more open to positive ones." He then spoke of his father, saying "He was weighed down, but the burden has been lifted. He needs to have more joy and it's right for both of them to feel it. I love them and want them to experience fun and joy again. I am not lost. I am always."

Elsie asked for clarification. Todd responded, "I am—that is not a past tense."

11/6/2000 3:00 a.m.

"Hello Elsie, It's me, Todd. Sorry, I wanted to give you some thoughts. It is about joy. It is a sense of being—a state, if you will. It is not something to expect, but something to strive for. Thank you for continuing to hear me."

12/3/2000

"Hi Elsie, It's me, Todd. Everybody is starting to get busy with the holidays and I can feel the love. That's the way I can be known. Feel the love—the energy. There is no focus on physical, but on the energy of spirit. Physical is only temporary. You always remember how you felt, don't you? That stays with you. Love is forever. Love is never ending. Tell my family I love them and wish all of them a wonderful holiday.

1/4/2001

"Hi Elsie, it's Todd. A message for Dad. Please tell him he's going to be ok, and let my mother know I do love the new babies." Elsie asked, "You love the new babies?" She wondered why he used the word "babies," because there was only one baby in the family. He responded with much emotion, "Oh yeah! I know that one is to come!" Shortly after their conversation, Elsie learned that Todd's sister was pregnant!

Sept/ 4/ 2002

The month of August had made Elsie reflect on the wonderful gift given through Todd, as it was the anniversary of when she first started receiving his messages. She had since heard messages from others and had spoken to her clergy about them. Upon their recommendation, she had become involved in the healing ministry at her church.

At the end of her daily meditation, she received a visit from Todd.

"Elsie, you are my friend, and I am your friend, Todd."

It was a surprise to Elsie as she hadn't heard from Todd in a long while.

Todd added, "Oh hi, yes, thank you for coming through. So much to ask of you—please pray for my dad." Elsie prayed and thought she could feel Todd praying with her. Then Todd added, "He will be better. Thank you for your prayer. God bless you, my friend. Thank you as always. Love to all." The departure was as swift as it had come.

Todd's mother shared with Elsie that September 15th was the anniversary of Todd's death and that she had hoped to hear a message from him on that day, but there was none. Elsie recommended that it might be helpful if she prayed for him to hear her and release him from the pull of her own need for him to "visit." If she assured him that his messages were comprehended, maybe he could move on to his other work. Then he could come in the joy of memories, and not in pain. Soon after, Todd's mother experienced two happy dreams of Todd: one as a baby and one as a small boy. It was reassuring to her to think that Todd had visited in her dreams. Todd's message of "Love to all," was his final communication with Elsie. His family remains forever grateful for his love, his messages and his encouragement to live their lives to the fullest.

From Todd's mother, Linda:

> When these messages were first relayed to me, I was in a very dark and bad place. I could not see a way forward through my grief and I had no desire to seek counseling because, honestly, a part of me didn't want to feel better. I wrapped my grief around myself like a blanket and I figured that this was the way

the rest of my life would be. That was fine with me because, while I would never have put my family through harming myself, I really didn't care much about life in general. I was sleepwalking through those first 10 months after Todd passed. I was acting all the time, and I was apparently a decent actor because I don't think anyone really knew how dark it was for me. I believed I would never feel joy again and I accepted that this was the way it should be; after all, the light of my life was gone; my best buddy and precious son.

When I first heard the words from my husband, "Your boy is trying to get in touch with you," I was very skeptical and remained suspicious for quite some time.

Shortly after the first batch of messages came through, I began what would become several years of individual, couples and group grief counseling. Today I try to live my life with as much joy and gratitude as possible. I want to live it FOR Todd, to honor the magnificent way he lived his own life. I believe that Todd, through Elsie, showed me the way to do this.

Todd and his sisters

A tribute to Todd from his mother, Linda:

Witty, handsome, thoughtful, loyal, loving, courageous, talented... I could go on, but these words only begin to describe the essence of my son & best buddy, Todd. Every mother believes her children are exceptional & wonderful, so that is no surprise, but Todd taught me & our family the true meaning of those adjectives as he fought with all his might through a grueling battle with Ewing's sarcoma. We prayed for miracles during those 18 months & while the miracle that we prayed for did not come, in hindsight, I see now that the miracle came in a different form than we had expected. It came in the way his sisters, nieces & nephews, over the years, have shown courage through their own battles with adversity. It came as his dad fought through his own battle with cancer & it comes every day for me as I strive to be strong, to carry on, despite my sorrow, for my family & friends. I want to feel every emotion; good, bad & sad because that means that I'm alive & have the privilege of feeling. In time I have learned to allow the emotions; loss, grief & sorrow to sweep over me like a warm blanket & I believe with all my heart that so much love cannot be lost. Love never dies.

*The Todd Bucher Foundation toddbucherfoundation.org raises money for sarcoma research at the Levine Cancer Institute and also sponsors pediatric cancer patients and their families during the holidays.

To make a donation by check, mail to:
The Todd Bucker Foundation
629 Beacon Knoll Lane
Fort Mill, SC 29708

Lauren
Full Angel!

Lauren was just a little girl when her Uncle Todd died. He was a teenager and, as expected, the family was devastated. Lauren remembers the family's grief and her own sadness, but because she was so young, she didn't completely understand the finality of the situation.

A few weeks after Todd's death, Lauren was getting ready for bed. She had a cheerleading event the following day. She missed her Uncle Todd and was upset that he wasn't going to be there to support her. She eventually fell asleep but awoke suddenly in the middle of the night. She wasn't sure if she was startled awake by a dream or if Todd "woke" her. She then recalls seeing Todd through her back window and she remembers being amazed as he "walked" through the window and into her room. "Full angel! He had wings and all!" She was calmed as he talked to her about her feelings and her fears. She felt comforted and soon fell back asleep.

A few weeks later, Halloween was approaching. Lauren was terrified of the spooky holiday. She always dressed up as a butterfly, a flower, or a fairy because she didn't want to be anything scary. She and her family had gone to a haunted trail that was hosted by a local Boy Scout troop. Her family didn't realize how frightened she was, but it was terrifying for her, especially when masked people jumped out from behind the trees. Later that night, when it was time to get ready for bed, Lauren went into the bathroom to take a shower. She had never been afraid to shower before, but on this particular night she was quite fearful that the creepy people from the haunted trail would be in the bathroom. As she got into the shower, she started crying. Then Uncle Todd appeared again. This time not in "Full Angel," but just as she remembered him- as a teenager. He told her that she would be fine and that none of the scary people could get her. He soon disappeared and an orb-like light appeared and moved in circles around the top perimeter of the shower. The orb stayed there until she finished showering, and then it disappeared. Again, Lauren was calmed and comforted by Todd's visit. She didn't realize that it was unusual to see people after they died.

The last time Lauren saw her Uncle Todd was about 5 years later. It was a difficult time for her family as her parents were going through a divorce. She remembers that she thought about Todd every day, but especially during that time. She needed his comforting personality to cheer her up. She remembers that she and her mother were shopping at a department store, and they were having a dreary day. She walked past the Men's section and saw her Uncle Todd standing there—plain as day in a red ECHO hoodie. He was smiling and bald, just like she remembered him. She instantly felt hopeful and reassured. Again, she felt very calm that he was there, and he was gone as quickly as he had come. He didn't speak to her during that visit, but his presence was all she needed to make her feel better.

Lauren's mom, Kristen, and the rest of the family were "blown away" when they heard about the visits from Todd. They were incredibly reassuring to each of them, and they knew they were tremendously comforting to Lauren at times when she needed Todd's support the most.

Although Lauren hasn't had any additional visits from Todd since then, she takes great comfort in knowing that he is near, and heaven is just a blink away.

Alison
You Have a Choice

Alison was overjoyed with the upcoming birth of her baby daughter. She was young and healthy, and the pregnancy had been uncomplicated. Plans were in place for a midwife to perform the delivery in the comfort of a nearby house that had been converted into a birth center. The day of delivery arrived, and everything seemed to be going smoothly, however, the labor was unusual in that instead of numerous smaller contractions, Alison had one enormous and very painful contraction. The baby girl was delivered, but she was blue and scored only a 2 out of 10 on the newborn APGAR scale that assessed whether she would require additional medical or emergency attention. Alison continued to bleed, and her midwife tried to expel what she believed to be a clot. Unfortunately, it was not, and the source of the persistent bleeding was actually a tear in the uterus. The midwife and her assistant tried desperately to stop the bleeding, but instead of improving, Alison began to hemorrhage. Although they were very close to the hospital, Alison heard frantic calls for an ambulance. By the time paramedics arrived, Alison felt an extreme peace about her. As the EMTs were attempting to stabilize her for transport to the hospital, Alison felt a sensation of hovering over the team that was now working diligently to save her life. She watched empathetically over the team as if she were a spectator invited to watch a harrowing medical drama.

One young paramedic looked very upset at what he was seeing, and she wondered if this was the first time he had ever watched a person die. He was doing his best to reassure her that she was going to be okay. She knew better. She recalls the surreal feeling of being wheeled out the back door of the birth center to a waiting ambulance. Things were moving quickly now, and she wanted to scream, but she could only manage a quiet whisper. When she arrived at the Emergency Department, a medical team converged upon her in an attempt to fully assess and start IVs so they could give fluids and blood transfusions to replace the blood she had lost. It felt overwhelming. She began thrashing about on the bed because she knew she was dying and didn't know what to expect on the "other side." As a mask was being placed on her face to give her anesthesia, her heart stopped beating and her heart monitor flatlined.

Suddenly she had the sensation that she was at the bottom of a deep well. Alison felt a spiritual energy leaving her body and a consciousness leaving her eyes. She felt like she was at the bottom of a tunnel looking up through a forest toward an umbrella of light. It was like the rays of light that can be seen coming through the trees, but significantly magnified in intensity. It was so beautiful and bright, but despite the incredible brightness, it was not at all painful or blinding. It was beautifully bright. She heard glorious voices singing and she felt bathed in happiness. She felt the energy and spirits of loved ones spiraling and projecting her up toward the magnificent light. The feeling was wonderful, and she knew this was where she was supposed to be. After rapidly ascending toward the light, she plateaued at the top. She felt a great force of light and love. She saw the most exquisite lights and colors—colors that are indescribable using words in our language. There were different spectrums of colors and they were so much more pure and beautiful than the colors in this world. There was no time reference, and she felt like she had been there forever. And then a thought came from a heavenly being in front of her, "you have a choice." She wondered what it meant. She couldn't remember what had transpired before she reached this magnificent place. Alison felt that she faced a very difficult decision. She felt disoriented. It was impossible to look away from the bright presence, but she felt something pulling her away. There seemed to be a very fine line between two very different places.

And then suddenly Alison was back in her body and everything looked and felt black. She was on a ventilator that was helping her breathe, but she was not in sync with the machine and was fighting to gain control of herself and her breathing. There was a nurse at the foot of the bed, but she was preoccupied and hadn't noticed Alison's struggle. She had been through a lot, but she knew she needed to try to calm herself down. A short time later the nurse noticed that she was awake and aware and summoned the medical team to evaluate her. In time, Alison was weaned from the ventilator and eventually discharged from the ICU. She had received 9 units of blood and every lifesaving act her medical team could perform to save her life. She was back.

Her baby girl was doing well, and Alison slowly healed and returned to her normal life. She would later learn that there were 7 or 8 people in that emergency room trying to bring her back to life. The physician in charge was an accomplished writer and spiritual leader. At the very moment Alison flat lined, the physician had instructed everybody in the room to pray. When she felt pulled to make a choice, the medical staff had been praying for her. They prayed for her to return, and they prayed for her life and the lives of her family.

Alison no longer takes her life for granted. She is thankful for every day she has on Earth. When she passes a car wreck, she prays differently than she used to and differently than most of us do. She prays for guidance for those involved, and she prays that they don't panic. She prays for whatever is best for them.

You can hear the passion in Alison's voice as she tells her story. She believes it happened to her for a reason and she feels compelled to share it with others in the hopes that it will change them in the same way it changed her.

Alison's tribute to her daughter, Cielle:

> *I have deep gratitude for the power of God which saved my beautiful daughter, Cielle's, life. I am so thankful for the influential people in her life, especially her*

father, her grandparents, and her brother, Trevor, who has always been her protector and guide. I am also so grateful for her Guardian Angel who has never left her side. I am so proud of Cielle and my heart is full as I watch the creative, artistic, passionate person she has become. She came to this Earth already knowing how to navigate life, and she has never slowed down. I pray this story gives others hope and inspiration as we all traverse this complex yet miraculous life together, knowing that what awaits us on the other side is pure love, bliss, acceptance and grace.

a note from author Kathy Lamm:

Alison's physician father and I worked in the same hospital. One day he and I were sharing an elevator ride and he asked if I would mind if his daughter, Alison, shadowed me for a day as she was interested in learning more about the PA profession. As she stood in my office looking at the many pictures on the wall, she was drawn to a picture of a little girl who was dressed in ruby slippers and a blue and white checked dress. She said she had to know more about the little girl, so we sat down and I shared the story about her visits to heaven. Alison looked at me with amazement and smiled. I assumed it was because the story was so beautiful. But it was more. She paused for a minute as she stared at the picture and collected her thoughts. She then proceeded to tell me about her own visit to heaven. It was amazing to me that an elevator ride with a physician I rarely see, a one-day encounter with Alison, a chance viewing of a photo on a wall, and a pull to one little girl in a picture led Alison to share her remarkable story with me.

I should mention that the picture she was so drawn to was of a little girl named Skyler...

Skyler
Glory, Glory, Glory, Hallelujah!

Diagnosed with leukemia when she was 5 months old, there was a well-worn path between Skyler's home and the children's cancer center. She would go into remission, stay a short while, and then relapse. Over and over again. It was heartbreaking and exhausting. When she was just 5 years old, the treatments stopped working altogether, and her doctor had the devastating discussion with her parents that they were out of options.

Skyler's mother, Jackie, had recently separated from Skyler's father, and Jackie felt alone in shouldering the stress of dealing with her daughter's terminal illness. She felt completely overwhelmed and couldn't bear the thought of a world without her beautiful daughter in it. And Skyler was terrified of dying. She had been told wonderful things about heaven, but she didn't really understand, and she didn't want to leave her mother alone in the world. Knowing how Skyler felt was almost too much for her mother to bear.

Over a several week period, Skyler's condition worsened. She stopped walking, ate almost nothing, and became painfully thin. For three days, she barely moved. Her mother carried her everywhere as the little girl was too weak to walk. She received continuous IV fluids to keep her hydrated and comfortable. Skyler was lying on the sofa, minimally responsive, when her mother took a break to go the bathroom. A minute later, Skyler appeared at the bathroom door, carrying her IV bag, excited and beaming. Her eyes were big and bright, and she was smiling as she said, "Mommy!" Jackie was speechless, completely stunned as she looked at the little girl who had barely moved in three days. She was dumbfounded. Was she dreaming? The silence was broken by Skyler's words, "I'm not afraid to die anymore!" She quickly went on to tell her mother that her "angel friend, Gabe" had just visited her. She described him as having "skin that was darker than mommy's" and "he was really tall with dark, curly hair." "And he was so nice." Jackie remained motionless as she continued to stare at her daughter in amazement. Skyler enthusiastically continued talking and told her mother that Gabe had invited Skyler to join him because he wanted to show her something. He then took her for a visit to heaven to show her how wonderful it was going to be. In heaven, Skyler was greeted by an angel named Marie! She paused and smiled at her mother, seemingly expecting a response, so Jackie asked about Marie. The little girl laughed as if her mother was trying to be silly. She said, "Mommy, you know Marie! She's your granny! She's been in heaven for 22 years!" Skyler had never met her great grandmother who was only ever referred to as Granny Stanley by family members. Jackie's hands were over her mouth as she processed the words she was hearing. How long ago had it been since Granny Stanley died? Having no idea, she ran to the phone to call her own mother. When her mother answered the phone, Jackie blurted out, "How long ago did Granny Stanley die?!" Her mother paused for a moment as she recalled the year and calculated aloud, "It'll be 22 years in May." Jackie was astonished at her mother's words. She stood speechless and shocked and hung up the phone without saying another word. How was any of this possible?? She then hurried back to Skyler to see if there was more to this incredible story.

Skyler was excited to continue. She told her mother how Marie had gently taken her by the wrist "like this" as she grabbed hold of her own wrist, and Jackie flashed back to how Granny Stanley had done the same with her when she was a little girl. Skyler went on to describe how Marie had shown her around heaven, with Gabe following closely behind. Jackie could tell that Skyler was fascinated with the beauty of heaven. The angels were "beautiful and huge," much larger than she thought angels would be. Their colors were amazing, and they wore the most magnificent gowns. She became frustrated when she couldn't explain how much more beautiful the colors were in heaven than they are here on Earth. As much as she tried, she just didn't have the words. The angel's colors and the colors of heaven were unbelievable. Heaven was wonderful. "And I have a horse in heaven!!" Marie had taken Skyler to see the horse that would be hers when she arrived in heaven. Skyler was thrilled!

Skyler's condition remained stable over the next few months, and she had frequent visits from other "Angel friends" who took her back to visit heaven. On one visit she got to meet Jesus! "He was so very kind to me!" She explained to her mother that, "He has white hair just like Gidget!", their poodle. "And Jesus has a horse, too!! He's white!" She was thrilled that Jesus also had a horse. She described that Jesus sat next to God "like this," and she motioned with her little hands that he was on God's right side. And she loved how the angels sang beautiful songs when Jesus walked through heaven. When the angels stood around God's chair, it looked like a rainbow because their colors were so bright and beautiful. Her inability to describe heaven's beautiful colors again frustrated Skyler, but the frustration was mild compared to the excitement of all she had seen. Among the many things that Skyler saw in heaven was a book. She knew it was important and Jackie's name was written in it.

After the several month reprieve, Skyler's condition declined again. One day, as Skyler and her mother were napping, Skyler woke up and said "Mommy, look!", as she pointed to the other side of the room. The ceiling fan moved slightly, but Jackie saw nothing. Skyler said, "You see 'em, mommy?" Jackie lied and said she saw them. Skyler replied, "I TOLD you!! I wouldn't lie to you, mommy!" Skyler was seeing angels. Shortly after that, Jackie carried Skyler toward the bathroom, pain pump in tow. As they made their way down the hall, Skyler said, "Oh! Oh! Mommy!" and then she started singing a song that Jackie had never heard before. Her sweet, angelic little voice sang, "Glory, Glory, Glory, Hallelujah." Jackie asked her about the song, and Skyler explained that it was the song the angels sing when Jesus walks down the streets of heaven.

When they returned to the couch, Skyler said, "When I'm in heaven my hair is long and pretty, and when I come back here, it's short." Jackie assured her that she was beautiful no matter how long or short her hair was. Skyler then said, "When I visit heaven, I don't hurt, and when I come back here, I do." What an unbelievable dilemma for a mother who isn't ready to say goodbye but doesn't want her child to suffer.

On the day she died, Skyler asked for her mother's permission to leave and go to live in heaven. "Mommy I've been thinking. I'd like to live with Jesus and my angel friends if it's okay with you." She said she had talked with Jesus, and He said he would take good care of Jackie after Skyler went to heaven. She added, "Mommy, I won't hurt there." She placed her tiny hands on either side of Jackie's face and asked, "Mommy, is it ok?" Jackie closed her eyes and prayed. She nodded her head up and down and choked out the words, "If that's what you want to do." She hugged her baby girl and Skyler said, "I'm going to live with Jesus tonight."

Skyler was at peace. She decided that she wanted to have a party. She made a list of the people she wanted to attend, and she told her mother that she knew what each of them should bring. Jackie got her paper and pen, and Skyler dictated her list. "Granny needs to bring ice cream, Momma a coloring book, Papa a superball, Daddy needs to bring pizza, the preacher should bring chicken "legs," Bubba a vanilla milk shake, and Sue and Bobby need to bring cake." She wanted party hats and "blow things" with Barney on them. The party was set for 7 pm. Skyler made her mother promise not to tell anybody about her plan to join Jesus that night.

Skyler ate more that night than she had eaten in days. She ate chicken "legs," drank her milkshake, and she laughed. She asked her guests, "How do you catch a unique rabbit? Unique up on it!" She was full of energy and was an entertaining hostess. The party was a huge success.

Shortly after her guests had all left, Skyler looked up at her mother with big eyes. She asked her mother to hold her, and Jackie snuggled up behind her girl. Skyler asked her mother to hold her tight. Jackie held her and felt Skyler take a deep breath. She took two more breaths and went limp in her mother's arms. Jackie said she could feel Skyler's soul leave her body.

As Jackie was planning the funeral, she remembered that Skyler had wanted to wear a white princess dress, white gloves and white ballerina slippers when she went to heaven. Jackie was able to find the white gloves and slippers, but she could only find a light green dress. She delivered the items to the funeral home. When she returned home, she found a little white dress hanging in a plastic bag on her front door. She hadn't shared Skyler's wishes with anyone, and when she asked family and friends about the dress, no one claimed to have left it. Perhaps one more gift from heaven?

Jackie will forever be grateful to Skyler's angel friends. She will always remember the comfort and amazement that Skyler felt after those visits to heaven... and the incredible peace they brought to both of them.

Skyler

Tribute from Skyler's mother, Jackie:

After I spent time with Skyler, I have no doubt we are all going to be together again. I am so thankful that God chose me, out of everyone in the world, to be her mom. As soon as I saw her in the hospital, I heard The Almighty's voice, "Take her, she needs you. This is the child I have for you." We had been praying for a child for many years. He was just saving the best one for me. Her adoption was final one month after she was diagnosed. But it was so worth everything to be able to be her mommy.

Acknowledgements

Thank you from Wendy:

To our patients (including Ella, Patsy, and Kim), colleagues (David, Sharon, Ann), the friends, children and parents who shared these wonderful glimpses into the other side. These special encounters that you have shared are amazing. We are so very grateful.

Kathy. Obviously. My co-author. My sister and my friend. Forever. We alone know the immense love of our childhood. The wonderful memories of birthdays and holidays that were always made special. The fall festivals and days at the pool. Vacations, cartoons and Incredible Edibles. Sometimes silly memories that mean the world to only us. Our immense love of animals. We are both so thankful that we still share our lives. We even live next door to each other half the year. We are so blessed. Kathy is the one that pushed us to do this book. I would have given up long ago. It was sometimes so frustrating. But we persevered. And I'm so happy we did. If we help give hope to even a few people, then it was worth it.

Our beta reader: Laura O'Bannon. Laura has read this book as many times as we have. Thank you for being so diligent and for catching so many things that we missed! And thank you for loving the animals with us!

Our Seal Team Members. Joanna Hunt-publisher extraordinaire -thank you for all your direction, support, and knowledge. Dyanne Simpson, DO, DFAPA, Corinna Muller, DO FACOOG, Laura O'Bannon, and Kaitlin Brick. You were all unbelievably helpful as you listened to our stories and gave us feedback. You also know our training and our secrets. Until our next assignment. Over.

To Kaitlin Brick. My heart. My daughter, my friend, my travel partner. My greatest joy. Your father and I are so blessed to be your parents. You are an amazing person, and you are so very loved. You make my heart full. Thank you for pre-reading and helping with story placement.

To my husband, Bob. Together since we were 16. Wow. You are the perfect partner in life. Thank you for always encouraging my ideas, even though some are crazy. Thank you for fostering my wanderlust and my love for all the creatures. You really get me. Right down to the center of my heart. Thank you for always being there, even when it's hard. I'm not sure it's possible to even describe how much you mean to me. I love you so very much. Truly, you are my everything.

To Ted and Carol Gram. Mom and Dad. Our wonderful parents. Thank you for being the perfect parents for us. You were always so loving, supportive, nurturing and loyal. We always knew that we were deeply loved and cared for. Our home was our safe haven. You gave us the perfect childhood and the perfect opportunity to succeed. You showed us how to love our families, our friends and the animals. Every single day, I thank God for you and your love, for the people you were. And I miss you so incredibly much. But I know we will see you again and that reunion will be amazing! Thank you, Mom and Dad. For everything.

Thank you from Kathy:

Thank you doesn't begin to say how much we appreciate everyone who shared their hearts and their stories over the years, and again while we were writing this book. Thank you for always being available to answer every single question so we could make this as accurate as possible. I know it was sometimes difficult to relive and discuss the memories, and I can't begin to express my gratitude to all of you.

Thank you most graciously to each of the parents and families who have lived through a cancer diagnosis and shared your battles, your journeys, and your beautiful stories. You are all my heroes, and I know your angels are so very proud of you....Jackie Trull Taylor, Linda Bucher, Chanda Courtney, Anita Elam, Angel (Roark) Ellington Cotton, Yvonne and Adlai Lowry, Barbara and Josh Jones, Lynn Roberts, Antoine, Keehanna and Jeremiah Avinger, Katie D, Cheri Benge Jones, Brigette Boteler Ray, Betty Lynn and Walter Scholtz, Lauren Arthur, and Elizabeth and Nils Martinsen.

Thank you, Sharon Breeding, CCLS, for sharing your story as well as Jillian's and Victoria's. You are one of the kindest and most compassionate people I've ever known, and it's no wonder the children love you so much. Bob Palmer (cart 1, seat 2), thank you for sharing Gene and Warren. I know their experiences have strengthened your faith and made you the person you are today. Thank you, Randy Germann, for introducing us to Chuck and reminding us that we don't have to be perfect, but if we have faith we will be "good to go!" Ann McKenney, thank you for sharing Punky with the children and with all of us. You are an absolutely beautiful soul. Thank you, Alison Sugg, for sharing your incredible story. I'm thankful you were "pulled back" so we could hear about your amazing visit to heaven.

Thank you, Jackie Trull Taylor, for sharing sweet Skyler with me all those years ago. Her story is what inspired me to write this book.

Thank you to all of the cancer and sickle cell patients I have had the privilege of working with over the years. What a blessing it was to hang out with you and your families.

Thank you, Kris Germann, PA-C, for encouraging this book for the past 25 years and for carrying the purple feather pen. To Dan McMahon, MD, Pediatric Hematologist/Oncologist, Wesley Stenzel, Gina Thornburg, Jennifer Riggall, BSN, Wendy Kilman, BSN, Amy Walters, Amy Warren, CCLS, Kathy Martin, PNP, and Amy Kelly, PNP—thank you all for your support and for sharing angel messages.

Thank you to our esteemed, elite, and hilarious Seal Team Author Group. To our book coach and publisher, Joanna Hunt, for keeping us on track, and for your guidance and expertise. To Corinna Muller, DO, FACOOG, and Dyanne "NTTGDD" Simpson, DO, DFAPA, for laughing and crying with us through the entire writing process. To our Beta readers- Laura O'Bannon (who can probably recite the book by heart at this point) and Kaitlin Brick- thank you for reading the unedited version and for your invaluable input. "ALOLA!!"

Thank you to my wonderful family- my husband, Doug, and my son, Alex. Thank you always for your love, support, and encouragement. I couldn't have done this without you. I love you both very much.

Thank you, Wendy, for being a great co-author, sister, and friend. After all these years we finally, FINALLY finished! It wasn't always easy, but I am so happy we persevered. We connected with so many amazing people, shed some tears, laughed a lot, and made it through. I'm so happy we did this together. I love you and have always felt so lucky to be your sister.

And lastly, I'm so thankful for our wonderful parents, Ted and Carol Gram, who gave us the most unconditional love and support throughout our lives. For a lack of better words, they were simply the best, and we knew even at a young age how blessed we were. I hope they are somewhere nearby where the colors are beyond our earthly comprehension, and they are proud of this book and the messages we are sharing.

www.ingramcontent.com/pod-product-compliance
Lightning Source LLC
Chambersburg PA
CBHW070834100426
42813CB00003B/614